GERMANY'S OTHER HALF

by Franz von Nesselrode

GERMANY'S OTHER HALF

*A
Journalist's
Appraisal
of
East Germany*

Abelard-Schuman

London   New York   Toronto

Photographs on jacket cover, reproduced courtesy of German Information Center, New York.

LONDON	NEW YORK	TORONTO
Abelard-Schuman	Abelard-Schuman	Abelard-Schuman
Limited	Limited	Canada Limited
8 King Street WC2	6 West 57th Street	896 Queen Street W.

Printed in the United States of America

Contents

GERMANY'S OTHER HALF

Part 1

**The German Land Behind
The "Chinese Wall"**

EAST GERMANY AND MIDDLE EUROPE

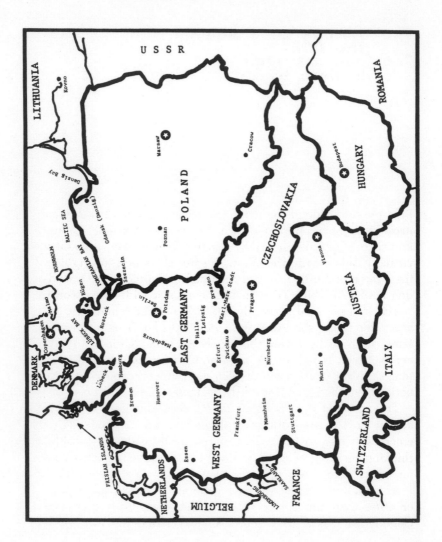

1

The DDR
Is Here to Stay

Like the dark side of the moon, East Germany, alias the "German Democratic Republic" (in German, "Deutsche Demokratische Republik" or DDR) remains, to this day, a country virtually unknown to the West. In spite of its position right in the center of Europe, it is a secluded and practically forbidden land — a white Tibet in the heart of a wide-open world.

Yet, in a physical sense, the DDR is neither remote nor inaccessible. What shrouds it from view have not been tall mountains, high walls (even the newly erected "Chinese Wall" across Berlin is not an insurmountable obstacle) or deep waters; rather it is a curtain of prejudice and preconceived false notions, overhung, as it were, by a dense political smog.

True, a great deal is being published about East Germany almost daily in the world press these days, but the picture that emerges is one so blurred by propagandistic design, wishful thinking, slanting of news and malicious comment that it conjures up a completely distorted view.

As the DDR has not yet been recognized by any great power other than the Soviet Union which gave birth to it and Communist China, itself still a country struggling for world-wide recognition, it is a land generally inhospitable to, and shunned by the press of the Western world. Even American correspondents who roam the four corners of the globe seldom visit it, and if they do, they usually limit themselves, or are limited, to a given area (such as the Leipzig Fair) that cannot provide a representative picture of the whole.

As a result, virtually all the news about East Germany available to public opinion in the West comes from either one of two tainted sources. One is the Bonn Government (and in particular its "Ministry of All-German Affairs") which is an interested party in the case, preoccupied with cold war propaganda and desperately intent on preventing the DDR from gaining international recognition in any form. The other is West Berlin which in recent years has been a hotbed of prejudice, rumor-mongering and all sorts of "intelligence" activities and which therefore appears as about the most unsuitable place for objective reporting one can think of.

Not that the news coming from the opposite corner is any better. It, too, is one-sided, self-centered and colored — as rose-tinted as that coming from the other side is black-hued. In short, neither German side can be trusted to tell the truth, or even merely to present a reasonably objective picture of what East Germany today is really like.

There is only one way — to go and find out for oneself, with a cool head, a minimum of preconceived notions, and a critical but not hostile mind, as the author of the present book believes he did.

Even so, any attempt to present a factual and unbiased account of conditions in the DDR is greatly handicapped from the start. Too many people still believe that books and articles about that country must be either pro or con. The writer who sets out to do a book neither for nor against the East German regime must be prepared for vituperation from both sides. And he inevitably will have to run the gauntlet of indignant critics brandishing clubs from the right, the left and the center.

The trouble starts right with the name of the country (but, is it a country? is it a state?) we are concerned with. Its official name evidently is a glaring misnomer. It has been said, with some measure of justification, that the "German Democratic Republic" is neither democratic, nor a republic, and not even German. It certainly isn't a democracy in the Western sense of the term, for democratic institutions and procedures as we know them are conspicuously absent from its public life. But, then, what the DDR really aspires to be is that weird product of Communist double-talk known as a "people's democracy." (The term would be a tautology if it weren't just plain nonsense.)

The Austrian Socialist leader Bruno Pitterman once gave a perfect definition of this linguistic misfit when he declared, "The difference between a democracy and a 'people's democracy' is exactly the same as that between a jacket and a straitjacket." Anyway, it is hard to quarrel with the official name a state has adopted for itself.

On the other hand the West Germans, who fear nothing more than the possibilty of the rival Communist regime some day gaining international respectability, apply all kinds of devious names to it, none of which is accurate. To persist in talking about the "Soviet Zone", or simply about "the zone," is pretty ludicrous in view of the fact that the occupation of Germany has ended long ago, and the country's division into zones with it. And, whether we like it or not, the DDR is an organized state that has been in de facto existence for over a decade.

Equally misleading is the term "Middle Germany," the use of which is being fostered by some Bonn officials and parts of the West German press, since it has irredentist overtones, the implication being that the real East Germany lies beyond the Oder-Neisse-Line in what now is Polish-administered territory.

Since it is practically forbidden in West Germany to give the eastern neighbor its official name — even the use of "DDR" in quotation marks or references to the "so-called DDR" is frowned upon — the German press and radio have only a choice between two misnomers, "the zone" and "Middle Germany." Outside of the Federal Republic, however, one need not bow to this semantic tyranny any more than one need accept "German Democratic Republic" at face value. The simplest way out of the dilemma is to use the abbreviation DDR or (in English) GDR, as is now widely done abroad.

Strictly speaking, it is just as incorrect to speak of "Pankow" when referring to the East German government. This term came into use because the presidential palace (now the official residence of the Chairman of the State Council, Walter Ulbricht) is located at Niederschönhausen, in the city borough of Pankow, in northeastern Berlin.

Actually, the seat of the government, in particular the chancellory of the Premier, the People's Chamber and all the principal ministries are located well within that central portion of Berlin (eastern sector) which has been traditionally the administrative headquarters of all central German governments since Bismarck.

Nevertheless, a case may be made for the continued use of "Pankow" on grounds of convenience, if only when reference is made to the two rival governments ("Bonn" and "Pankow").

As the Western world is veering away from the use of the inept term "Soviet Zone," the question of whether and to what extent the DDR should be recognized is also receiving more thoughtful consideration. Heretofore, the official approach to the East German problem prevalent in Washington (and only in slightly less degree, also in London and Paris) has sprung from a mixture of total ignorance, wishful thinking, half-hearted interference and the mouthing of pious platitudes. Its gist seemed to be to look upon the East German state as a hideous freak not to be touched with a ten-foot pole but also one that surely would go away or fall apart some day if only we kept our fingers crossed, prayed hard and kept the secret service mills turning.

A more sensible approach now at last appears to be in the offing. It starts out with the premise that the present East German regime, illegitimate and unpalatable as it may be, is an established fact to reckon with. Having been in power, in one form or another, for more than 17 years, it is not likely to disappear or to be drastically changed in the foreseeable future.

For the DDR, as constituted today, is an integral part of the Soviet orbit and nothing but the forcible overthrow of the Communist regime in Russia could conceivably bring about its collapse. Indeed, the only remote possibility of bringing about a change of political conditions in East Germany (barring total war) would seem to be through some form of confederation with the Federal Republic. This, however, is a most unlikely contingency, since the Bonn Government is averse to any kind of union with the DDR, except on its own terms. In effect Chancellor Adenauer and his supporters expect unconditional surrender from a foe which is not only undefeated but solidly entrenched and shielded by the greatest military power in the world. This kind of statesmanship is the best guarantee of a long life for the undemocratic regime in East Germany!

Whether we like it or not, it is an undeniable fact that the East German regime, since the abortive uprising of June 17, 1953, which rocked it but could not bring it down, has gained considerable strength in at least two respects: 1) Economic conditions have greatly improved, both in terms of the standard of living and with regard to industrial production and foreign commerce; and 2) There is a definite, world-wide trend towards diplomatic recognition of the DDR, if not on a de jure then at least on a de facto basis.

In the first eight years of its existence as a more or less nominally independent state, the East German republic was held in an iron ring of diplomatic isolation due to the so-called "Hallstein Doctrine"; i.e., the declared intention of the Bonn Government to break off diplomatic relations with any country (other than the Soviet Union) that would establish such relations with the DDR.

This threat was effective for a long time because the Federal Republic, with a population nearly three times as large as that of East Germany, and a booming economy that made conditions on the other side of the demarcation line look drab and shabby, appeared as a far more attractive partner to do business with.

Although a number of non-Communist countries even then contrived, by various devious means, to do a little business with the DDR and still stay in the good graces of the Bonn Government, this diplomatic quarantine by and large held good until the fall of 1957. On October 15 of that year, however, the "cordon sanitaire" which Dr. Hallstein had thrown around East Germany was breached decisively when Yugoslavia extended full diplomatic recognition to the DDR.

Yugoslavia, which has demonstrated time and again that it is not taking any orders from Moscow, in this instance took the realistic position that two German states exist and that both should be recognized. Yet Bonn, jealous of its previously unchallenged status as the sole legitimate and representative authority in Germany, would not see it that way. It immediately broke off diplomatic relations with Yugoslavia, hurting in the process German trade and German good will most. To date, diplomatic relations between Yugoslavia and the Federal Republic have not been restored.

Belgrade's example had a strong impact especially on the

non-committed nations of Africa and Asia. Both Syria and Egypt promptly followed suit to the extent of organizing "trade missions" in East Berlin that lacked the attributes of diplomatic representation only in a very formalistic sense. In 1962, Iraq did the same. The principal reason why these Arab countries did not establish formal diplomatic relations with the DDR must be seen in their fear of retaliatory recognition of Israel by West Germany.

Since then the DDR has achieved a good deal more progress in its steadfast bid to become a socially acceptable member of the family of nations. Besides maintaining full diplomatic relations with all the members of the Soviet bloc (to wit, the USSR, Poland, Czechoslovakia, Hungary, Bulgaria, Rumania and Albania in Europe; the Chinese People's Republic, North Korea and North Vietnam in Asia) as well as with Yugoslavia, the DDR at present maintains official trade missions in the following non-Communist countries:

United Arab Republic (Egypt)	Ghana	Yemen	Argentina
Syria	Guinea	Sudan	Colombia
Lebanon	India	Laos	Uruguay
Iraq	Burma	Cuba	Finland

In addition, semi-official trade missions (ostensibly accredited by the East German "Chamber of Foreign Commerce") have been established in Belgium, Denmark, France, Greece, Indonesia, Iceland, the Netherlands, Norway, Austria, Sweden and Turkey.

The United Arab Republic, Guinea and most recently, Iraq so far have taken the boldest steps towards outflanking the "Hallstein Doctrine." A full-dress DDR consulate-general was set up in Cairo on September 24, 1959; another in Damascus early in 1961. The same happened in Baghdad on June 16, 1962. (See also chapters 24 and 25.)

At the "summit conference" of nonaligned nations, held at

Belgrade in September, 1961, East Germany's bid for international recognition was carried a big step forward. Although the conference refrained (at the insistence of Indian Prime Minister Nehru) from including in its final communiqué a passage recommending the de facto recognition of the DDR, it is known that the large majority of participants favored such a move.

"With very few exceptions," wrote *Die Welt* of Hamburg editorially on September 7, "the statesmen present there (at Belgrade) have expressed views similar to those of Moscow with regard to the Berlin and Germany questions. In some instances, they unreservedly supported the Kremlin stand in these matters."

The same paper, in an earlier report from Belgrade by its special correspondent Peter Grubbe, had candidly summed up the situation as follows: "In future, the only way to stop de jure recognition of the (Soviet) zone will be to pay for it in cash. Let's face this truth brutally."

One could of course engage in endless debate on the merits or demerits of recognition on legal and moral grounds. Certainly East Germany's moral prestige is low. There is no arguing with the fact that the DDR is a state set up by the will of the Soviet Military Administration, and that it has never demonstrated, through free and honest elections, that its government is representative of the people's will.

However, if East Germany — the same as all other Soviet bloc countries — is a thinly disguised dictatorship, so are any number of charter members of the so-called free world, in particular Spain and Portugal. The "democratic" government which the Central Intelligence Agency in 1954 installed in Guatemala was just as spurious and a product of naked force as the government of the DDR — and even less popular at that. Yet it was "recognized" by most countries after the fact, and without qualms.

No real progress towards a lasting international settlement can be made as long as we go on withholding recognition from solidly established governments on account of their ideological makeup and political allegiance.

As Walter Millis wrote in *The New York Times Magazine* of February 2, 1958: "The establishment of Communist regimes in China, North Korea, North Vietnam and in Central Europe is the result of historic processes which, whether good or ill, cannot be undone by any form of power available to the West; we should accept the situation and learn to live with and deal with it rather than indulge in counter-revolutionary hopes and propaganda which are futile to begin with and ill become the greatest of the conservative and *status quo* powers."

This is the voice of reason, and it applies to East Germany even more than to Red China and other Asian countries. For, in contrast with the bellicose Chinese, the Ulbricht regime has never indulged in any kind of military venture or taken any action designed to disturb the peace of the world.

Even in West Germany, the winds of change are beginning to blow in the direction of common sense. Witness the editorial "Schach dem Kanzler" (Check to the Chancellor) in the influential weekly paper *Die Zeit* of September 22, 1961, in which the political editor, Countess Marion Doenhoff, wrote: "... Our make-believe foreign policy has been running for years on two rigid tracks: The Hallstein Doctrine and the rule that all negotiations mean appeasement... One of the most prominent businessmen in this country recently told me, 'When I feel that the future of my firm is threatened by competitors ... I sit down to negotiate with them and try to work out a modus vivendi or at least an arrangement to prevent the worst. If I had practiced in my field policies like those the Chancellor pursues on the highest level, I would have gone bankrupt long ago.'"

In the case of the DDR, the wise French saying "Il n'y a que le provisoire qui dure" (only temporary things last) has again been proved to the hilt. Like its counterpart in the West, the DDR had been conceived as a provisional, stop-gap creation. By now, however, it has already been in existence as long as Hitler's "Thousand-Year-Reich", and even much longer counting its embryonic period as the Soviet zone of occupation.

Make no mistake about it: the DDR is here to stay. And, since it is sure to be with us for a long time to come, we might as well get acquainted. Let us therefore try to peer through the political smoke screen that has been shrouding this country for so long and take a long, hard look at the realities that lie behind.

2

The DDR:
A Primer of Basic Facts

Area and Population

The DDR, as presently constituted, covers an area of 107,834 square kilometers or 41,635 square miles with a population of 17,079,306 as of January 1, 1962.

Its territory is divided into 14 Districts, plus the eastern sector of Berlin which, in spite of still being under four-power rule in a nominal sense, has been, to all practical purposes, incorporated into the DDR. Indeed, Berlin is officially considered as the capital of the country; all chief administrative departments are located there.

SIZE AND POPULATION OF THE DISTRICTS (1960 Figures):

	sq. kms.	Population
Rostock	7,068	829,708
Schwerin	8,642	629,467
Neubrandenburg	10,896	660,668
Potsdam	12,413	1,173,619
Frankfurt	7,049	658,662
Cottbus	8,208	805,653

SIZE AND POPULATION OF THE DISTRICTS   (1960 Figures):

	sq. kms.	Population
Magdeburg	11,525	1,390,354
Halle	8,765	1,981,215
Erfurt	7,306	1,256,974
Gera	3,994	728,845
Suhl	3,853	545,203
Dresden	6,740	1,894,745
Leipzig	4,964	1,531,019
Karl-Marx-Stadt	6,008	2,127,003
(formerly Chemnitz)		
East Berlin	403	1,085,030
	107,834	17,298,165

The DDR is one of the comparatively few countries in the world whose population, in spite of a normal excess of births over deaths (in 1959, there were 16.9 births and 13.3 deaths per 1,000 population), has been decreasing steadily in recent years. By official count, the total population of the country was 18,388,200 in 1950; 17,832,200 at the end of 1955; 17,603,-578 on December 31, 1956, 17,298,165 at the end of 1959, 17,188,488 at the end of 1960 and 17,079,306 by latest count, as noted before.

This striking and seemingly unnatural downward trend is solely accounted for by the movement of refugees to the West. Since 1949, when the DDR was established, a total of almost three million persons have fled to the Federal Republic. In view of the fact that in 1960 again almost 200,000 persons migrated westward and that this exodus continued in the first half of 1961 (103,159), and at a greatly accelerated rate in July and early August of that year for a total of 188,000, it is not surprising that the present population of the country, including East Berlin, has fallen to just over 17 million.

As in Western Germany, there is a substantial surplus of

women. Of the 17.3 million persons living in the country at the start of 1960, over 9.5 million were females and under 7.8 million males.

It is interesting to note, though, that this female surplus, which is of course in large measure due to the ravages of the two world wars, relates only to persons above the age of 26 and is particularly heavy in the age groups 30 to 70. Below 25, the statistical picture shows a slight but steady excess of males over females which is most marked in the age groups 1 to 10.

PRINCIPAL CITIES OF THE DDR	1960 pop.
East Berlin	1,082,349
Leipzig	592,821
Dresden	483,515
Karl-Marx-Stadt (Chemnitz)	286,226
Halle (Saale)	278,700
Magdeburg	260,618
Erfurt	186,066
Rostock	155,351
Zwickau	129,394
Potsdam	115,163
Gera	100,924
Dessau	93,273
Schwerin	92,195
Görlitz	90,658
Brandenburg (Havel)	86,862
Jena	80,835
Plauen	79,743

In 1959, 71.7% of the total population were classed as city dwellers (including all towns of more than 2,000 inhabitants) and 28.3% as rural population living in communities of less than 2,000.

The country's cultivated area covers about 6.5 million hectares or 16 million acres, 4.9 million hectares (12 million acres) being arable land; 2.9 million hectares (7 million acres) are forest.

Natural Resources

The DDR is a highly industrialized country with a comparatively weak energy base; it is heavily dependent on imports of foodstuffs and industrial raw materials which are paid for by the finished products of its engineering, chemical, optical and other industries.

Hard coal, abundant in West Germany, is very scarce in the DDR. The only major deposit is in the Zwickau area of Saxony and total reserves there are estimated at only 40 million tons. Annual output is less than three million tons and production is becoming costlier and more difficult as deeper layers have to be mined. Large quantities of hard coal, therefore, must be imported, chiefly from Poland but in part also from West Germany.

By contrast, brown coal or lignite is available in enormous quantities. Total reserves are estimated at 40 billion tons, or 1000 times as high as those of hard coal; at least 25 billion are fit for industrial use. As there is practically no oil or natural gas — some minor deposits have recently been discovered but they have not yet been developed — and comparatively little water power, the bulk of the energy used in the country comes from brown coal.

Of the electric power produced in 1959 (37,248,023 million watt hours), no less than 89% was derived from brown coal fuels (71.5% raw brown coal; 7.2% briquettes and 10.3% coke); 4.4% was generated by hard coal and 4.3% by gas. Water power accounted for 1.4% and mineral oil for only 0.2% of the total.

While the output of brown coal is scheduled to rise by 29%

in the course of the current Seven-Year-Plan (1959-1965), the East German planners expect to have at their disposal, in 1965, five times as much crude oil as in 1958 — some of it from domestic sources but mainly through massive imports from the Soviet Union.

As a result, oil, of which six million tons annually will be available beginning in 1965 if all goes according to plan, will account for about 9% of the DDR's raw energy balance, as compared with only 2% in 1958-59.

The Plan provides for an output of 278 million tons of raw brown coal in 1965, as compared to actual production of 214.8 million tons in 1959. (For further details about the role of brown coal in the East German economy see Chapter 9.)

Metallurgy

There is little iron ore in the DDR and it is of comparatively poor quality with an iron content of about 25%. In 1959, 395,136 tons of iron ore and 25,559 tons of copper ore were produced in the country. The output of pig iron (based mainly on iron ores imported from the Soviet Union and coal imported from Poland) amounted to 1,898,422 tons in 1959, that of crude steel to 3,207,437 tons.

The principal ironworks are at Stalinstadt (q.v.) and Maximilianshütte, (usually referred to as "Maxhütte") while the chief steel mills are at Hennigsdorf (Berlin), Riesa, Brandenburg and Gröditz; there are additional steel rolling plants at Hettstedt, Burg and Olbernhau, among other places. High quality steel ("Edelstahl") is produced at a special plant at Freital, not far from Dresden.

The Chemical Industry

With a total of 1,114 plants of all sizes (including 163 major ones, all nationalized, which account for 93% of current production) the chemical industry, in the DDR, is one of the mainstays of the national economy. Its share of 14.8% in total industrial production is larger than in any other country.

As an export article, chemicals rank second after machine-building in the DDR. Foreign sales in 1959 were valued at 1.2 billion marks, an increase of 200 million over the preceding year. Synthetic rubber, plastics, artificial fertilizer, insecticides, photo and motion picture film, pharmaceutical products, soda and tires made from synthetic rubber are some of the chief export articles.

Among the most important chemical plants are the Leuna Works "Walter Ulbricht;" the Buna Chemical Works at Schkopau; the Bitterfeld electrochemical combine; the dyestuffs factory of Wolfen; the Agfa Wolfen film plant; the Coswig plant (sulfuric acid and superphosphates); the "Friedrich Engels" Works of Premnitz (artificial silk).

Machine-Building

This is the most important industrial sector in the DDR which at present accounts for more than 30% of total industrial production (the term, as used in German, includes heavy engineering, electrical appliances, machine-tools, agricultural machinery, motor vehicles, ships, aircraft and many other items). It is also the one that earns more foreign currency through exports than any other.

Among the principal enterprises in this field are: The automobile works of Eisenach (Thuringia) which since 1955 has produced the popular small car "Wartburg", which comes in various forms and shapes (as a coupé, sedan, limousine, station-wagon and sports car). Annual output is about 30,000 cars. (While I was in the DDR, in June 1961, I came across a news story that said a total of 200,000 automobiles, including 135,-000 "Wartburgs", had been turned out at Eisenach since 1945.)

Another, smaller plant, the "Sachsenring" of Zwickau, manufactures the "Trabant," a smaller and less attractive model (present output: 20,000 a year). A small number of luxuriously equipped official limousines, type "Sachsenring", are also produced there.

Trucks are no longer made in the DDR but are imported from other Soviet bloc countries, especially Hungary, under a COMECOM (Council for Mutual Economic Aid) arrangement aiming at a maximum of specialization in each country of the bloc.

Generally speaking, motorization in East Germany, while it has made substantial progress in recent years, is still far behind West Germany, except in agricultural machinery. To some extent, the scarcity of passenger vehicles is compensated by a rich assortment of motorcycles (1959 output: 87,000) and "mopeds" (161,200); they are produced mainly at Zschopau. The five Baltic shipyards, described in Chapter 21, also account for much machine-building.

The city of Magdeburg is the center of heavy engineering. All types of machinery, except motor vehicles, are produced in this area; small ships are also built there. Electromotors are manufactured at the Wernigerode Works in the Harz Mountains, among other places. Optical and precision instruments are manufactured mainly at the famous Zeiss Works of Jena; radios and television sets at Dresden; electronic equipment in both these cities and elsewhere.

Light Industry

This term, as used in German, covers the textile and garment industries, shoe production, woodpulp and paper and the manufacture of all kinds of consumer goods, including the much-discussed "thousand little things" which of late have been receiving, in the DDR, belated and much-needed attention.

By far the most important center of the garment industry including hosiery is Karl-Marx-Stadt (formerly Chemnitz) in Saxony. Cotton fabrics are also produced at Dresden, wool-

ens and carpets at Gera, lace at Plauen and various types of
nylon (perlon, prelon, lanon etc.) at Premnitz, Schwarza,
Spremberg and other places.

Hirschberg, Seifhennersdorf and Eppendorf are major centers of the leather and shoe industries. Incidentally, the output
of all types of shoes, in the DDR, is slightly higher than in West
Germany (3 against 2.4 pairs annually per head of the population), but the quality is poorer and there are fewer leather
shoes than in the Federal Republic.

The Building Industry

Although new apartment blocks are springing up everywhere and building proceeds apace at a high degree of industrialization and standardization (cf. Chapter 7), the housing
shortage persists; it is hardly worse than in West Germany,
though. In 1959, 65,561 new dwelling units were finished, as
compared to 48,468 in 1958. Present plans provide for the construction of an additional 772,000 apartments with modern living space for 2.5 million people, until the end of the current
Seven-Year-Plan in 1965.

Agriculture and Food Production

Farming is, and probably will remain for some time, one of
the weakest spots in the DDR economy. Why this is so will be
explained in detail in two subsequent chapters.

In the gross national product, agriculture, including forest-
ry, accounts for only 9.9%, against 65.3% for industry (5.8%
for building, 5.6% for handicrafts, 4.9% for transportation and
7.6% for commerce).

Here are some recent figures on crops and livestock: In 1959,
5,947,598 tons of cereals of all kinds were harvested, 3,503,158
tons thereof for human consumption (1,370,620 tons of wheat
and 2,132,538 tons of rye) and 2,444,440 tons of fodder.

Other farm produce, in 1959, included: 12.4 million tons of

potatoes; 4.6 million tons of sugar beets; other beets used for fodder, 7.8 million tons; corn (maize), 6.1 million tons; hay, 3.3 million tons.

Livestock, in 1959, included: 4,464,800 heads of cattle (thereof 2,157,500 cows); 8,283,000 pigs; 2,114,600 sheep; and 38,604,200 poultry.

Mechanization of agriculture is making good progress. In 1959, there were 41,680 tractors in use (against 37,076 in 1958), plus large numbers of sowing and harvesting machines.

How Much Private Enterprise?

Ever since the inexorable process of nationalization began with the arrival of the Red Army in 1945, the private sector in the East German economy has been shrinking fast. For a long time, industry was the main target of the socialization drive, but since the middle of 1960, when the collectivization of agriculture was completed in a four-months "crash program" (cf. Chapter 13) it has been only second in the field.

According to official statistics, 46.6% of all industrial enterprises were still privately-owned in 1959, as compared with 32.3% that were owned by the state and 21% listed as "mixed", i.e. private but with state participation. A very different picture, however, emerges if we look at it from the angle of output volume. For, the state-owned enterprises accounted for 88.9% of gross industrial production, while the private firms shared in it with only 5% and the mixed ones with 6.1%.

State-owned enterprises, in the DDR, are called VEB's (from "Volkseigene Betriebe" or People-owned plants). They are grouped together in vast trade associations called VVB's (from "Vereinigungen volkseigener Betriebe").

In handicrafts and small trades, as in domestic commerce, the private sector is somewhat larger. In 1959, 84% of all craftsmen were still doing business on their own, while 16% were organized in cooperatives. In commerce, the cooperatives led with 44.7%, against 34.9% state-owned enterprises and a private sector of 20.5%. Construction is 63.5% in the hands of the state, 10.5% in those of cooperative societies, while 18.9% of it is still done by private and 7.2% by mixed firms.

The entire economy is strictly controlled by the State Planning Commission in Berlin, a huge administration. Formerly, all planning was done in five-year periods, but in 1959 the seven-year-system was adopted in harmony and close coordination with the planning of the other Soviet bloc members.

3

The Powers-That-Be

The DDR has been officially defined as a "workers' and peasants' state" and as a "people's republic." The Constitution of May 30, 1949, declares in Article 3 that "all power derives from the people."

According to Article 50, "the highest organ of the Republic is the People's Chamber (Volkskammer). In Article 63 it is — or was — stipulated that the Chamber elects the President of the Republic (this office no longer exists), supervises the Government and appoints the Supreme Court judges. In theory, laws are passed either by the People's Chamber or directly by the people by means of a national referendum (in practice, this never happens).

The strongest parliamentary group in the People's Chamber nominates the "Ministerpräsident," or Prime Minister; he forms the Government (Art. 92). Under Article 101, a President of the Republic was to be elected at a joint session of the People's Chamber and the Chamber of States for a four-year term. Since then, however, the "States" have been abolished and the office of President, too.

All this sounds quite democratic, but the practice is different.

tive for the SED to say that it is the Communist Party, that it is running a dictatorship of the proletariat and that it will not give up an ounce of power until its goals have been attained. What makes it so difficult even for the best-intentioned to give full credit to the SED leaders for their real accomplishments in many fields is precisely this loathsome masquerade with a multitude of purely nominal parties, the constant misuse of the term "democratic" and the general hypocrisy of the political structure.

From the day the DDR was set up the head of the government as "Minister-präsident" or Premier has been the former Social-Democrat Otto Grotewohl. Grotewohl was leader of that faction of his party which in 1946, under strong pressure from the Soviet Military Government, agreed to merge with the Communists in the "Socialist Unity Party."

Since November 1960, Grotewohl, suffering from an unspecified ailment, has not exercised the functions of the premiership. His virtual retirement was confirmed when Stoph became Acting Premier in July 1962 (see below).

The real key figure of the administrative setup, however, has from the start been Walter Ulbricht, veteran Communist leader, who in 1946 became First Secretary of the SED and has held that job ever since. While there never was any doubt that Ulbricht, rather than Grotewohl or anyone else in the country held the reins of power firmly in his hands, he contented himself for a long time with the post of First Deputy Premier under Grotewohl. This fiction was discarded on September 12, 1960, when the People's Chamber, after the death of the first President of the Republic, Wilhelm Pieck, abolished this figurehead office. Instead it established a new super-administrative organ, the State Council, with Ulbricht as chairman. Significantly, most of the other 23 members of the Council are little-known party hacks, Ulbricht being the only figure of note in the setup.

The sweeping powers with which this Council was endowed by the legislature — including the right to rule by decree and to issue "binding interpretations" of existing laws — have made it crystal clear, even outwardly, that Ulbricht is the top man of the regime. (Cf. Chapter 5)

Key members of the Cabinet, as constituted in the fall of 1961, are:

WILLI STOPH, who became Acting Premier on July 7, 1962. Previously he had been First Deputy Premier, and head of the Central State Control Commission which supervises all governmental activities on behalf of strong man Walter Ulbricht and his party. Stoph is a comparative newcomer who made his debut on the political scene in the early fifties, then quickly rose to important posts. His first Cabinet post was that of Interior Minister in 1952; in 1956 he became Minister of Defense.

KARL MARON, Minister of Interior and in that capacity head of the redoubtable "People's Police" (see below); he is an old Communist party horse.

LOTHAR BOLZ, Minister of Foreign Affairs and Deputy Premier. He is a representative of the National-Democratic Party in the Cabinet.

BRUNO LEUSCHNER, President of the State Planning Commission since 1952, is the chief economic policymaker of the regime. Early in July, 1961 he was named Deputy Premier in charge of economic coordination. KARL MEWIS, hitherto secretary of the SED in the District of Rostock, then took over as head of the State Planning Commission.

Another top economic administrator was HEINRICH RAU, long-time Minister of Foreign Trade, who suddenly died on May 23, 1961.

HILDE BENJAMIN, Minister of Justice and only woman member of the Cabinet (another woman, GRETA KUCKHOFF, is president of the Central Bank).

GENERAL HEINZ HOFFMANN, another Communist of long

standing, became Minister of Defense in July, 1960, succeeding Willi Stoph.

MAX SEFRIN (CDU) and PAUL SCHOLZ (DBD) are the principal representatives of their respective parties in the Cabinet, both with the rank of Deputy Premiers. The representative of the LDPD, HANS LOCH, no longer appears as a Deputy Premier on the latest Cabinet list as he did before.

In connection with the appointment of Willi Stoph as Acting Premier, a minor shakeup of the Cabinet took place. Two State Secretaries (Undersecretaries) were dropped and six new Ministers were named to portfolios of secondary importance.

Apart from the political support it draws from the tightly knit SED and the mass organizations controlled by it, the regime relies primarily, in its bid for perpetual power, on the two armed props, the "Volkspolizei"or People's Police and the "Nationale Volksarmee" or National People's Army.

While the People's Police is as old as the regime itself (including its embryonic period 1945-49), the National People's Army is a more recent creation. It did not formally come into existence until January 18, 1956.

According to Western intelligence reports, the National People's Army, at the beginning of 1961, had an active strength of 110,000 men and a reserve of 130,000.* There are two armies each comprising three divisions and equipped with 1,800 modern heavy and medium tanks of Soviet make.

The naval arm, called "Volksmarine" or People's Navy, consists of seven fleets and about 400 mostly small warships. It is reported to possess four destroyers, seven submarines, and 22 minelaying and sweeping vessels. Its present strength is 12,000 men.

---

*According to a statement made early in 1962 by Army General Heinz Hoffman, Minister for National Defense, the active strength of the National People's Army was 90,000 men.

The Air Force is made up of two fighter squadrons with
400 planes including about 200 MIG jets. Of the 13,000 members of the Air Force, 1,200 are trained pilots.

A thinly disguised form of universal military service was
introduced on September 20, 1961, when the People's Chamber passed a law empowering the State Council (i.e. Walter
Ulbricht) to declare a "state of defense" whenever he deemed
the country in danger of attack from the outside and to draft
all able-bodied citizens into service "for the defense of the
republic or the protection of the population." A full-dress law
on conscription followed on January 24, 1962.

While there is little doubt that the National People's Army
represents an efficient fighting force — German armies of
whatever political color usually are — its complete devotion
to the regime is doubted by many observers. However, the
fact that in recent years most of the professional officers inherited from the days of the Nazi Wehrmacht have either died
or been retired should give pause to those West Germans and
Western military men who like to indulge in a bit of wishful
thinking about the East Germany Army in the event of conflict joining the Western side.

All of the top military leaders in East Germany today boast
a revolutionary background and many of them had fighting
experience in the Spanish Civil War. For instance, the Minister of Defense, Heinz Hoffmann, holder of the highest military rank (Army General), is an old-time Communist (born
1910 at Mannheim) who served as a political commissar with
the 11th International Brigade in Spain.

Deputy Ministers of National Defence are: Admiral Walde-
mar Verner, head of the East German Navy; Lt. Gen. Heinz
Kessler; Maj. Gen. Kurt Wagner; and Maj. Gen. Rudolf Men-
zel.

According to a statistical survey recently published by the
East Berlin Government, 85% of the Army's officers, from lieu-

tenant to general, are of working class descent, 12% are classed as "employees," and only 3% have been drawn from other professions. Among non-commissioned officers, the proportion of workers and peasants is even higher (93%) and in the lower ranks it amounts to 83%.

Judging by these figures, the National People's Army, by this time, must be one of the most heavily indoctrinated branches of the executive and, on the whole, reliable from the viewpoint of the regime. To be sure, there have been defections to West Germany (the other way around, too!) but they do not appear to be heavy enough to prejudge the issue of loyalty.

In any event, the Ulbricht regime does not depend for its survival on the loyalty of any of its citizens. It is protected by the military power of the Soviet Army, the strongest in the world. As long as that great power remains unbroken, the DDR is reasonably safe from internal upheaval as well as from outside intervention.

4

Thumbnail History
Of the DDR

The "German Democratic Republic" came into being on October 7, 1949, on the strength of a proclamation sponsored by the Soviet Military Administration in the territories of five "Länder" or States (Saxony, Thuringia, Mark Brandenburg, Saxony-Anhalt and Mecklenburg which at the time made up the Soviet zone of occupation).

On the same date, a provisional People's Chamber was constituted. On October 10, this body, with the concurrence of a provisional Chamber of States ("Länderkammer"), elected Wilhelm Pieck, then the Number 1 leader of the SED (and previously of the German Communist Party), as President of the Republic; at the same time Otto Grotewohl was named Premier. He has held this position ever since.

The new state was recognized, October 15 to 25, by all Soviet bloc countries, but by no other power.

The first cracks in the state structure soon began to appear. On February 8, 1950, a "Ministry for State Security" was formed for the specific purpose of dealing with enemies of the regime as well as with spies, saboteurs and other foreign agents. A secret police that came to be known as SSD (from Staats

Sicherheits Dienst or State Security Service) was organized under the authority of this Ministry.

In its first major foreign policy action, the new government, on June 6, 1950, signed a pact with the Polish Government formally recognizing the Oder-Neisse-Line as the permanent "peace frontier" between the two countries. (The West German Government steadfastly refused to accept this document as a valid treaty binding on the German nation).

On February 23, 1952, the original five Länder, including the historical states of Saxony and Thuringia (the other three were postwar creations of the Military Government), were abolished and the country was divided into 14 administrative districts.

The Soviet Control Commission was dissolved in May, 1953, its functions being transferred to a High Commissioner of the USSR in Germany. In March, 1954, the High Commissioner's Office was abolished in turn as Moscow granted "complete sovereignty" to the government of the DDR. The state of war between the Soviet Union and Germany ended formally on January 1, 1955, though a peace treaty has not yet been signed.

Meanwhile, on June 17, 1953, the regime was rocked by an unexpected internal revolt. In a way, it was an odd time. Vladimir Semyenov, the Soviet general and new High Commissioner as of late May, was known to be of more liberal disposition than his predecessor. Too, Premier Grotewohl proposed a "new course" that would ease a number of unpopular measures — regarding travel restrictions between East and West Germany, persecution of clerics, crop quotas, pressures against the middle class and private enterprise.

Grotewohl's new course was adopted by the Government on June 9. But on June 16-17, aroused by an increase in work norms by ten percent in the midst of still acute shortages of food and consumer goods, workers demonstrated first in East Berlin, later in Leipzig, Magdeburg, Halle and other major cities.

Farmers joined by protesting against the collectivization drive. Property losses were high, and there was widespread rioting and some bloodshed. But with the aid of Soviet troops and tanks, the uprising was quickly brought under control.

On the political scene, the most spectacular result of this upheaval was the removal from office of the Minister of State Security and head of the SSD, Wilhelm Zaisser. He was succeeded by Ernst Wollweber.

On May 14, 1955, the DDR formally joined the Warsaw Pact group as an independent and sovereign member.

A new wave of unrest followed the uprisings in Poland and Hungary in the fall of 1956. Now it was the intellectuals rather than the workers and peasants who took up cudgels against the dogmatic and narrow-minded Ulbricht regime.

In November, 1956, what was officially described as a "student's plot" was crushed by the secret police. Prof. Wolfgang Harich of Humboldt University in East Berlin was subsequently identified as ringleader of the conspiracy, as alleged by the regime; on March 9, 1957, he was sentenced to ten years' imprisonment at hard labor.

In August, 1957, Soviet Premier Nikita Khrushchev paid a state visit and heaped high praise on Walter Ulbricht (previously there had been reports of friction between Ulbricht, a Stalinist of the purest obedience, and the not-so-Stalin-loving Khrushchev). A currency reform took place on October 13, 1957.

A new "purge" of malcontents and dissidents within the Socialist Unity Party was carried out by the party's central committee at its 35th plenary session on February 3-6, 1958. Again, the Minister of State Security, Ernst Wollweber, was one of the targets; another was Karl Schirdewan, until then "Kaderchef" (chief of personnel) of the party. They were charged with various forms of "deviation" from the party line and of seeking to reestablish intellectual freedoms of the limited type granted to the Poles under the new Gomulka regime. The up-shot of the inquisition was that Schirdewan was expelled from both the Politburo and the central committee of the SED; Woll-weber (who had already resigned as Minister of State Security on November 1, 1957) was also expelled from the central com-mittee (he had not been a member of the Politburo). A third leading party member, Fred Oelssner, was dropped from the Politburo but retained his ZK membership.

At the Foreign Minister's Conference in Geneva, in June, 1959, the DDR, with powerful help from the Soviet Union, ob-tained its first taste of international recognition when its rep-resentatives were admitted as observers on a par with those from Western Germany.

On October 1, 1959, the People's Chamber decided to adopt a new national flag for the DDR (black-red-and-gold, as in the Federal Republic, but with a hammer-and-compass insig-nia added to these colors), thereby symbolically deepening the split between the two German states and making division more permanent.

The death, on September 7, 1960, of President Wilhelm Pieck, after a long illness (he was 84), opened the way for the assumption of virtually unlimited powers by Ulbricht. At his prompting the People's Chamber decided to abolish this large-ly decorative office and to set up instead a 24-man State Coun-cil with real powers, whose head was to become, by the same token, Chief of State.

To nobody's surprise, the Chamber elected Walter Ulbricht, who until then had been only the Number 3 man in the state hierarchy, to this post. In assuming the chairmanship of the Council, Ulbricht in fact leapfrogged over his former superior, Premier Grotewohl, who now "discharged" him — at his own request — from the deputy premiership.

With the additional powers granted him by the People's Chamber on September 20, 1961, under which he may at any time declare a state of defense and thereafter "rule the rights of citizens and the law in the need of the defense of the republic in deviation from the Constitution" (as a Reuters dispatch from Berlin translated the unwieldy German text), Ulbricht's ascendancy was complete. From then on, he was and is running a one-man show in the DDR as much as Khrushchev does in the USSR — if not more so.

5

The Man Who Runs
The Show — Walter Ulbricht

East Germany's strong man, Walter Ulbricht, 68, is a much-maligned person. To the West German press which, with comparatively few honorable exceptions, does not show much more inhibition in dealing with prominent political figures across the line than do the East German Communists, he is the devil in person. He has been charged with everything from having been a pimp and brothel-keeper in his youth (a lie, based on malicious gossip that has long since been disproved but nevertheless keeps going around) to being a would-be Communist Hitler. The latter accusation, which has been bandied about with increasing frequency since the East German regime closed the intra-city border in Berlin on August 13, 1961, is absurd to the point of idiocy. Indeed, one could hardly think of a greater dissimilarity in personality, character, outlook and general behavior than between Hitler and Ulbricht.

Herr Ulbricht is no Führer type at all, even though he now may wield (under the enabling act referred to in the previous chapter) sweeping powers which even the sedate *Christian Sci-*

ence Monitor on September 22, 1961, described as "Führer powers." Far from being an enthralling rabble-rouser like Hitler or Mussolini, Ulbricht is a most uninspiring leader. Of all the evil, or supposedly evil, world leaders to whom he has been likened, he probably comes closest to the picture of his former boss and idol, the late Joseph V. Stalin. But even there differences exist.

"Ulbricht is a bureaucrat and he always will be," a man intimately associated with him some thirty years ago once said, and his prophecy proved even more correct than his statement of fact at the time. He was Ernst Thälmann, the long-time leader of the German Communist Party who was imprisoned by the Nazis and died at Buchenwald concentration camp in 1944.

Ernst Thälmann statues and monuments today can be found all over the DDR, and the streets and squares that have been named after the dead Communist leader are legion. All this would seem to testify to a close personal relationship between Thälmann and Ulbricht. But the historical truth is different.

Even if one dismisses as unsupported and malicious gossip the thesis of some former Communists now living in Western Germany (they are, as usual, among the bitterest critics of the East German regime and animated by intense personal hatred against Ulbricht) who claim that it was Ulbricht himself who tipped off the Gestapo to Thälmann's secret hideout, the disturbing fact remains that the former did nothing to help his jailed friend.

He could have done so, at that. For at the time of the short-lived, but temporarily intense Hitler-Stalin collaboration in 1939, Ulbricht was living in Moscow and was very close to the Soviet dictator, while Thälmann was in a Nazi concentration camp. If Ulbricht really had wanted the then top leader of the party to go free, his good friend Stalin at that time might have been able to arrange for an exchange of prisoners or he

could have simply ransomed Thälmann out of jail. But Ulbricht
then was on his way up to the top and apparently was in no
hurry to see Thälmann at the helm of the party again.

No matter what his former comrades and sworn enemies of
today may say of him, or what the propaganda mills in Bonn
and West Berlin would want the world to believe about him,
Ulbricht is not Satan incarnate. As a matter of fact, he is rather
a well-intentioned person who sincerely aims at the better-
ment of working class conditions and who has the preserva-
tion of peace very much at heart.

If he is at times ruthless and tyrannical in a bureaucratical
sort of way, he is far from being a bloodthirsty despot like
Hitler. Ulbricht so far has shed very little blood, if any; he
makes a practice of sparing the lives of his fallen opponents,
or he simply shunts them off to unimportant jobs. In this regard he is far more humane than his former mentor Stalin.

Walter Ulbricht is the very prototype of the party "functionary", as they say in Europe or, to use an expression more familiar to Americans, of the entrenched machine politician. In
the dog-eat-dog world of Communist Party politics, he has
evinced a remarkable flair for the chances of survival. Whereas today in the Soviet Union, Poland, Czechoslovakia, Hungary, Rumania, Bulgaria, indeed almost everywhere in the
Soviet bloc, there is hardly a single leader left in power who
already held sway in 1945, Ulbricht at present is as much in
charge in East Germany as he was 16 years ago.

This achievement is the more remarkable as he has changed
his tactics very little. Long after Stalin's death and even at
the time when Soviet boss Nikita Khrushchev was firing Stalin-
ists right and left in the satellite countries as at home, Ulbricht
stubbornly and unashamedly clung to his Stalinist faith. In
the ideological dispute that has been going on in recent years
between Moscow and Peking, Ulbricht has barely concealed
his sympathy for the Chinese view. (This does not mean that

he believes in the inevitability of war as a prerequisite to world revolution as Mao and his supporters do; but rather that he favors the tough Chinese line in dealing with the West.) And it is certainly not by chance that Albania, that little rascal now virtually banished from good Communist society on account of its ideological affinity with Peking, is still getting more economic help from the DDR than from any other member of the Soviet bloc.

It is not true, therefore, to suggest (as for instance *Time Magazine* did in a typical "hatchet job" on Ulbricht in its issue of August 25, 1961) that Ulbricht is a "weathervane." Nor is he a Moscow "puppet" in the sense usually applied to him by the Western press. That he is an "agent" of Moscow — to use the slightly more courteous formula now coming into vogue in State Department pronouncements — cannot of course be doubted.

Ulbricht's outstanding characteristics are diligence, zeal, tenacity and a dogged determination to reach the goals he has set for himself and his party, regardless of cost or experience. He is a demon for work and he keeps plodding ahead along the chosen path even after all his companions have dropped by the wayside. In this respect he is very much like his arch-enemy, Chancellor Konrad Adenauer of the Federal Republic. In fact, the two men have quite a few things in common — their wooden faces, their unquenchable thirst for power, the way they drive themselves and their subordinates, their tactical skill and their political ruthlessness, among others.

Physically, Ulbricht is not much of a success. With his balding head, his wispy gray moustache and goatee, supposed to be a "Lenin-beard", his steel-rimmed glasses perched in school master fashion on a sharp nose, and his comfortable paunch, he is a boon for cartoonists who (in the West, anyway) are wont to heap even more scorn on him than do the editorial writers, and that is saying a lot.

Flora Lewis, writing in *The New York Times Magazine* of February 1, 1959, aptly described Ulbricht as having "the look of a small-town dignitary who has stumbled into the big world and is determined to hide his confusion." Only I feel it would be even more appropriate to speak of a "small town teacher" or "small town bookkeeper" than a dignitary.

Walter Ulbricht's life story is as humdrum and unexciting as the man himself. He was born on June 30, 1893, at Leipzig, the son of a tailor. As a youth, he learned the carpenter's trade and to this day he speak of himself as a carpenter by profession.

He is not, thus, a typical son of the working-class, as his admirers are fond of telling us (for instance, the late Johannes R. Becher who was Minister of Culture in the Grotewohl Government, in his 1958 biographical essay "Walter Ulbricht – ein deutscher Arbeitersohn"). Tailors and carpenters are craftsmen and they have traditionally belonged, in Europe anyway, to the small bourgeoisie rather than to the proletariat.

Both parents were militant Social-Democrats – a party far more radical in those days than nowadays – the mother even more so than the father. Even as a small boy, Walter was fed well-heaped spoonfuls of Marxism every day. He liked the heady brew and grew up with it. No sooner had he learned his ABC's than he began to read editorials from the local Socialist paper, the *Leipziger Volkszeitung,* to his illiterate father.

At the tender age of eleven (according to Joh. R. Becher) he was so steeped in political passion that he once burst into tears as he read to his parents a story in the paper about a strike that had collapsed.

Having left school at 14 to become a cabinet-maker's apprentice, Walter Ulbricht sought to improve and continue his education by joining a "Bildungsverein" or educational association organized by a Social-Democratic youth group at Leipzig. He was one of the eager beavers of the circle and apt to be seized with "intense emotion" (says Becher) as he declaimed Goethe's "Prometheus" to rapt listeners in the group. At the age of 17, young Ulbricht was bitten by the *wanderlust* bug. He donned a corduroy suit and heavy boots, put a Tyrolean hat with feather on his chubby head and, with rucksack and walking stick, set out on foot to see the world in the time-honored fashion of young German craftsmen ("wandernde Gesellen") in the good old days before motorization.

He roamed through Germany, Belgium, Switzerland and even made his way across the Alps into Italy. An earnest and studious young man, he spent much more time reading books, visiting museums and studying the monuments of architecture than in youthful frivolities.

Back home again, he attended evening classes on literature, pedagogy and other subjects; he also learned shorthand. With all these extracurricular activities in addition to his carpenter's work, young Ulbricht found time for athletics and sports. He joined the workers' athletic league "Eiche" (Oak) at Leipzig and, as always, became one of its most active members. Even today, in his late sixties, Ulbricht, in spite of his paunch, still is far more fit physically than most men of his age. He still enjoys swimming and skiing and is a good tennis player as well.

Even before World War I, Ulbricht had become a minor party functionary at Leipzig. He impressed his comrades with a skillful display of his modest oratorical talents and the vast fund of knowledge he had acquired at evening classes and on his trips abroad. He also wrote essays and theses.

There was a considerable to-do at the "Deutsche Bücherei" (National Library) of Leipzig recently when a librarian discovered by chance, in some musty archives, a lengthy paper Walter Ulbricht had written in those days on the subject of "Origins of the German Reformation," apparently for the purpose of gaining admission to an institution of higher learning.

The exact fate of "Origins of the German Reformation" is

not known; it seems the author himself has forgotten about it. But there is an amusing side to it. In the margin of the yellowed manuscript, a workmanlike, even scholarly job, the hand of an unknown critic has written the annotation: "This paper is so perfect in content and form that I am inclined to doubt very much that the author has not been guilty of cribbing".

At the age of 23, Ulbricht chucked his trade to devote his full time to party activities. When the Social-Democratic Party after the 1918 Revolution split up, Ulbricht followed the radical left wing into the newly founded German Communist Party.

Although he was one of the founders of the party — at any rate he was present at the meeting in 1920 where the K.P.D. (*Kommunistische Partei Deutschlands*) was organized — Ulbricht then was still too young to play a foreground role in the new party. He was outranked by Wilhelm Pieck, Ernst Thälmann, Klara Zetkin and others. Before long, however, he had risen high in the party councils in his persistent, plodding way, by dint of hard work and cunning.

His value to the party lay especially in his undisputed talents as an organizer. Hence also his code name "Genosse Zelle" (Comrade "Cell"), for he was an expert in the kind of underground political warfare requiring the fragmentation of large party units into tightly-knit direct action cells.

By 1928, Ulbricht had become a member of the Reichstag on the Communist ticket. As usual, he made full use of his privileges, such as the right to travel free in first class on the national railways, while other, more "class-conscious" Communist deputies, including party leader Thälmann, preferred to ride in the proletarian third class.

After Hitler's rise to power, Ulbricht was sent abroad by the party leadership, while Thälmann remained in the country (it is not quite fair to say that Ulbricht "was one of the first to run out", as *Time Magazine* did; all Communist leaders were under strict party discipline and the executive committee decided which ones were to go abroad and which ones were to stay).

He went first to Prague and later to Paris. After the outbreak of the Spanish Civil War, he was sent to Spain by his party to serve as "political commissar" on the Republican side.

His Spanish job ended, Ulbricht in 1937 went to Moscow where he remained till the end of the war. Among the many German Communist leaders who had sought refuge there during the Nazi regime, the bitter factional wrangles which had already torn the party before 1933 continued and were intensified by the party strife within the Bolshevik party itself.

In those days many of his former comrades deserted Ulbricht and one of them, the fierce Klara Zetkin exclaimed: "May a benevolent fate prevent this man from ever rising to the top of the Party. I cannot stand him. Look into his eyes and you will see how sly and false he is."

However, Ulbricht remained in the good graces of Stalin and that was all that really mattered. In 1943 when a number of turncoats among the many German officers captured at Stalingrad and elsewhere banded together in the "National Committee for a Free Germany," Ulbricht was given the job of organizing, and lecturing at so-called "antifa schools" (antifascist schools) where the German prisoners underwent reorientation courses. No one among the teachers at these schools was more intent on proselytizing the former Nazis than was the unsmiling, bespectacled "principal" that most of the students had never heard of before — Walter Ulbricht.

The war was not quite over yet when Pieck, Ulbricht and a number of other party bigshots on May 2, 1945, flew in a Red Army plane from Moscow to conquered Berlin and immediately set about reorganizing the German provinces that had been overrun by the Red Army in accordance with Stalin's directives.

A year later, the revived K.P.D. merged with the left-wing Socialists headed by Otto Grotewohl in the "Socialist Unity Party" or SED, as has been related before. By that time, the first big steps towards the establishment of a "Socialist economy" in East Germany had already been taken with the wholesale property expropriations of Nazis and war criminals (who happened to own most of the big industrial enterprises earmarked for socialization), and the sweeping land reform that wiped out the Junker class.

Many other drastic measures were to follow as the years went by. Nothing now could stop the purposeful and dogmatic little man who as First Secretary of the SED held the levers of power in his chubby hands, while co-chairmen Pieck and Grotewohl shared the public honors.

As he grew older, Ulbricht became more domineering and more, rather than less, intolerant. He set the pace at his own discretion, brooked no opposition and would bark orders in the tone of a sergeant addressing a company of raw recruits. That he did so in the broad, soft dialect of his native Saxony, which tickles German ears even more than does Adenauer's Rhenish dialect, only resulted in his orders being carried out with snickers behind his back.

With characteristic caution, Ulbricht did not move himself immediately to the top when the East German state was formed in October 1949. Undoubtedly he could have done so, for at the time Stalin's word was still the law everywhere in the Soviet orbit, and Ulbricht was Stalin's man.

But the path that lay ahead for the fledgling DDR was untried and untested; nobody could tell for sure where it would lead. So Ulbricht installed the aging Pieck, once a firebrand revolutionary but now a meek old man on the verge of senility, as President of the Republic, and he made Grotewohl Premier — i.e. the official responsible if anything went wrong. For his part, Ulbricht contented himself for a while with the deputy premiership which allowed him to be on the inside yet also in the background when he felt like it.

Relations between Ulbricht, the Moscow-trained Communist, and Grotewohl, the ex-Social-Democrat, have never been easy. Grotewohl himself, in an address to the party's central committee in February, 1958, frankly defined them in these terms: "We are two people who will not let personal differences become a cause for political conflicts . . . What would become of the German workers' movement if there were men at the top who would betray the cause of socialism for the sake of personal disputes?"

On July 12, 1957, the Associated Press distributed a curious dispatch from Berlin that read in part: "The Stalinist rule of Walter Ulbricht, boss of Communist East Germany, tottered today under the backlash of the Moscow purge. Reliable East Berlin sources said Ulbricht, Communist Party secretary, has come under attack within his own Central Committee . . . The informants said 'liberal Communists' are looking for some gesture of approval from Soviet Party Chief Nikita Krushchev to put spade-bearded Ulbricht on the skids.

"The West Berlin newspaper *Der Abend* quoted Communist sources as saying two members of the East German Politburo — Heinrich Rau and Karl Schirdewan — have broken with Ulbricht. The gathering revolt within the party was sparked by Khrushchev's purge of Stalinist V. M. Molotov and Lazar Kaganovich, who were closely linked with Ulbricht . . . Ulbricht made the mistake over the last months of indicating that he expected Molotov and his associates to come out on top in the Kremlin struggle for power . . ."

As happens so often with American news dispatches from Germany, especially about the DDR, this story was on the whole correct in reporting facts, yet at the same time it arrived at a totally wrong conclusion. While it accurately put the finger on Schirdewan as an opponent of Ulbricht (and the same was also true, though in lesser degree, of Rau), the inference that the rule of the Stalinist boss was "tottering" was wholly unwarranted. As a matter of fact, the Ulbricht regime has not come anywhere near to "tottering" since it survived the upheaval of June 17, 1953, and it appears to be now more solidly entrenched than it ever has been.

Khrushchev, though he may not be overly fond of Ulbricht, or of his extreme Stalinist views, has never given any indication of wanting to replace him with another man or set of men. If he ever harbored such thoughts, he abandoned them quickly after the Hungarian revolt, which led to a general tightening of reins within the Soviet bloc. Regardless of whether Khrushchev was sincerely working towards a liberalization of policies in the Sovet Union, it has been amply clear all along that he favored strongman rule in a satellite country so vulnerable and exposed, and at the same time so strategically important to Moscow as is the DDR.

Any illusions the dissidents in East Berlin may have had about getting help from Khrushchev in their struggle with Ulbricht were dashed thoroughly when the Soviet leader in August 1957 visited Berlin and showered signs of affection on Ulbricht and associates.

When the Soviet government delegation arrived in East Berlin on August 7, *New York Times* correspondent Harry Gilroy cabled: "Mr. Khrushchev at once disposed of rumors that Walter Ulbricht . . . might be out of favor because of too persistent loyalty to Stalin. The Soviet party leader gave Herr Ulbricht a warm embrace when they met in the main East Berlin railroad station. The two political leaders exchanged cordial greetings in speeches that followed . . ."

If any further confirmation were needed that Ulbricht is Khrushchev's man, just as he was Stalin's, it was provided by the apparent ease and total lack of outside interference with which he early in 1958 disposed of the growing opposition within the party.

The story is told that Schirdewan, at a Kremlin reception in 1956 after Khrushchev had made his famous anti-Stalin speech, had buttonholed the Soviet Premier and asked him with a wink in the direction of Ulbricht:

"You've gotten rid of your Stalin. Now what about ours?"

To which Khrushchev is reported to have replied cryptically: "Everything in its time."

The story may be true or apocryphal. If it happens to be true, Ulbricht's time has been a long time in coming.

And it still isn't here.

Part 2

I Saw the DDR in Action

(Reporters Notebook)

DISTRICTS:

1 Rostock
2 Schwerin
3 Neubrandenburg
4 Potsdam
5 Frankfurt
6 Cottbus
7 Magdeburg
8 Halle
9 Erfurt
10 Gera
11 Suhl
12 Dresden
13 Leipzig
14 Karl-Marx-Stadt
15 Demokratisches Berlin

Place names shown with stars have received special treatment in the text because of their novel or symbolic importance in East Germany today. These are, running north to south, *Rostock-Übersheehafen* (see ch. 20); *Schwedt* (see ch. 12); *Stalinstadt* (see ch. 10); *Schwarze Pumpe* (see ch. 11); and *Bautzen* (see ch. 18).

6

Who Says
They're Starving?

"Die Zone hungert" (The Soviet Zone is Starving), screamed the excited headline, in bold black and red letters, in *Bild-Zeitung*, West Germany's biggest mass circulation newspaper.

I rubbed my eyes in amazement. For, only a few days earlier, I had come back from a ten-day trip through the DDR, in the course of which I had been given ample opportunity to acquaint myself with current living conditions in that country; to visit scores of cities, towns and villages from Rostock to Bautzen; to talk with people in all walks of life; and, above all, to see with my own eyes, at my discretion, what is right and what is wrong in that secluded land behind the "Iron Curtain".

And, would you believe it? The most salient impression of all I gathered during my stay in East Germany was that the people over there were not only well-nourished, but that they were, indeed, grossly overfed.

Now, I realize that this statement will sound preposterous to Americans and Englishmen who read almost daily in their papers that these poor, down-trodden East Germans have been fleeing to the West by the thousands in order to escape the untold miseries of life under Communism.

Let me explain. In the first place, I am not disputing the fact that the exodus from East Germany, which has been going on steadily ever since that territory was occupied by the Red Army and forcibly converted to Communism until the Berlin loophole was closed by the "Wall of Shame" erected on August 13, 1961, has far outpaced the movement in the opposite direction. Nevertheless, a forgotten fact should be restated here: some 700,000 West Germans migrated or fled to East Germany between 1945 and 1962, according to official DDR figures.

Nor would I deny in the least that the mere fact of about three million people having left the Soviet zone or DDR during the same period proves that a lot of people living there are malcontents anxious to seize any chance of getting out from under.

Generally speaking, I am far from suggesting that life under the Ulbricht regime is sweet or that the East Germans are well off and have no reason to complain. If a good deal of what the reader will find in the present report is rather on the favorable side,the reason is not that the author, for sinister reasons, is trying to paint a rosy picture, but rather because there *are* praiseworthy accomplishments in the DDR that are hardly ever mentioned in the world press.

What I am trying to do, in this report, is not to depict the DDR as heaven on earth, or as the workers' paradise which Ulbricht and his party expect it to become some day, but merely to set the record straight and put a grossly distorted picture back into focus. For, world opinion has been for years deliberately and persistently misinformed about conditions in "the zone" for obvious reasons.

Indeed, the great bulk of what was and still is being published in the world press these days about conditions and happenings in the DDR comes from questionable sources. The most voluble fountainhead is the Bonn Government which lays claim to being the sole legitimate authority for all of Germany and which, therefore, looks with a jaundiced eye on all that goes on under the rival regime. The outpourings of Bonn's "Ministry of All-German Affairs" — whose prime reason of existence is to undermine the Communist regime in the DDR by fair means or foul — are all too often taken for gospel truth in the West, regardless of their manifestly one-side, partisan and biased nature.

Nor is there much objectivity to be found in the West German press. With few exceptions, the newspapers of the Federal Republic are as prejudiced and crassly partisan in their approach to the "Soviet zone" as is the Bonn Government. Hardly do they bother to check the "facts" they get from official sources or from their armchair correspondents in Berlin, to try to see things in the right perspective, or to take a peep at the other side of the coin.

Much of the "news" about Eastern Germany comes also from the dozens of secret services, underground organizations, psychological warfare agencies, etc., operating out of Berlin. Although the daily brew of misinformation concocted by these cold war specialists ad hoc in order to justify their existence is as ill-smelling as can be, it is gobbled with enthusiasm by a majority of the foreign as well as the West German correspondents stationed at Bonn or Berlin.

The regrettable fact that there are no American newsmen permanently stationed in East Germany and that very few of those "covering" that area from West German bases ever make even a fleeing trip across the demarcation line also helps blur the picture. Every now and then an American reporter will spend a couple of hours in East Berlin or take a plane hop to the Leipzig Fair, but that is as far as it goes, usually. In many of the places I visited, on my recent tour of the DDR, I was told I was the first foreign reporter ever seen in those parts since the War.

The long and the short of it all is that world opinion learns about East Germany only what is unfavorable and can be used for cold war purposes. The dark side of everything is heavily accented, while no attempt is made to include also the brighter side of things in the picture.

If, therefore, a great deal of what is described in the present report may come as a surprise, or even as a shock, to the reader, it is not that I am inventing things or dreaming up visions of the future, but rather that what is there has been kept from public knowledge in the West by overzealous propagandists.

A personal note may be in order here. I hold no brief for Communism in any form or shape. I am, and always have been, a democrat and a liberal. My recent hosts in East Germany are well aware of this. We had plenty of heated arguments and I gave tit for tat whenever I felt like it, which was often.

However, while I am basically a liberal democrat, I am an independent in politics. I refuse to cooperate in any cold war schemes and I will not distort the facts, as I see them, to accommodate "our side". The things I describe in the present book I have seen with my own eyes; according to the case, I have touched them, tasted them. They are no mirage. I deal in facts, and I tell the truth.

There may be another objection. What if I have been hoodwinked? If I have let myself be taken in by cunning stage-setting? If I have been looking at "Potemkin villages" and thought they were the real thing? If I mistook window-dressing for the real goods?

If anyone thinks I am that naive, let me tell him that I have been a newspaperman for some 35 years and that the old hands in this business aren't exactly gullible. Moreover, I went into East Germany with wide-open eyes, a mind filled with a healthy dose of scepticism, and prepared for all the propaganda tricks and legerdemains in the world.

To come back to where we started from, the startling fact of the matter is that I have never seen, in any country, as many people — men and women, but not children, I ought to add — who were conspicuously and even grossly overweight, as I noticed in the DDR. Nor have I seen in a long time so much over-eating, so many people gorging themselves just for the fun of it.

But, perhaps all these fat people I have seen in East Germany were government officials and party bigwigs? Perhaps the excellent food I tasted was available only in a few selected restaurants out of bounds for the common man? Or, it was served only on special occasions and was sure to disappear from the menu the moment the foreign visitor was gone?

Nothing of the sort. I have taken my meals in a score of restaurants, in a dozen or more different cities and towns, villages and factories. While prices varied (the mostly state-owned and operated restaurants in the DDR are divided into four different price classes, plus a "luxury" class), the food was uniformly plentiful and good. I always scanned the menu carefully, picked out at random what caught my fancy and invariably got what I had ordered; and it usually was, in quantity, quality and price, equal to what one would get in a comparable establishment in Western Germany. Even granting that in a few cases — for instance at my hotel in East Berlin or in Leipzig — my hosts may have arranged for special service, this could certainly not have happened everywhere. For, several times it was I who suggested we go to a given restaurant or café I had noticed and on one occasion I ate, or at least ordered food, all by myself in a popular restaurant I had gone to alone after I had had dinner with my companions elsewhere. I did so not because I was still hungry — in fact, I hardly could swallow a bite of this second dinner for being so full already — but merely for the purpose of finding out for myself what kind of food was being served in a restaurant where my coming could not possibly have been expected.

I remember most vividly one café at Bastei, a popular resort in the beautiful mountain country near the Czechoslovak border which is known as *sächsische Schweiz* (Switzerland-in-Saxony). We drove out there, on the spur of the moment, one

Sunday afternoon when there was nothing else to do. Although it was a huge place, every table was packed with customers. All around me, I saw people splurging on food and drinks as though it were their last meal. Some women actually were gulping down three difference slices of layer cake and a big serving of whipped cream on top. And they were paying the penalty of such gluttony, too! Indeed, I have never seen anywhere more obese people per square yard than in this place. On a rough count, I figured that at least 16 out of every 20 persons in that café were overweight.

However, the conspicuous and indeed shocking corpulence of the East Germans does not prove that they are living in an economy of plenty. On the contrary! One of the principal reasons why people eat so much in the DDR is that there is so little else to buy! A wide range of consumer goods on which the West Germans spend a substantial portion of their income, such as cars, television sets, refrigerators and the like, are in short supply in the DDR. On the other hand, there is plenty of cash in circulation. Wages and salaries are good, rents are extremely low, education and medical care is free. So a lot of people, not knowing what else to do with their money, just eat it up, literally.

There is another nutrition problem which also adds to the rising problem of national obesity (to the Government, which must pay for slimming cures, it is also a financial burden): people not only eat too much generally, they also eat the wrong things. While the consumption of bread, potatoes, meat, fats, pastry and similar heavy foods is enormous, causing periodical breakdowns of supply lines and resulting in sporadic shortages, fish, fresh vegetables and fresh fruit are generally scarce. Many elements of a healthy diet are unobtainable because they have to be imported from abroad and the government frowns on the importation of foodstuffs, preferring to buy industrial raw materials instead.

The only food item still rationed officially is potatoes. However, quite a bit of indirect rationing takes place whenever seasonal or local shortages occur, which happen quite often. Thus it has been noted that in the summer months a scarcity of certain meats as well as butter has been making itself felt regularly over the past few years, ever since large-scale official rationing was abolished. The same thing, apparently, happened in the latter part of 1961, after I had left the DDR, and again, in intensified form, in the spring and summer of 1962, if there is any substance to the spate of recent news reports about current food shortages in the DDR. It is possible, therefore, that certain foodstuffs which I had seen in ample, or at least sufficient, supply — not only in restaurants, but also in the many butcher shops, dairies and grocery stores I visited — became scarce again a few weeks after my departure. Still, I feel quite certain that most talk about people going hungry in the "zone" is sheer nonsense.

One last remark about food supplies. I was surprised at the large number of self-service stores and even American-type "super-markets" that are to be found in the DDR today, and I was impressed by their well-stocked shelves and neat appearance. In the super-markets, perishable foods were kept fresh in deep-freeze counters and customers were supplied with wire baskets on wheels for their shopping, just as in the United States. Shelves were stacked high with canned goods, much of it imported from other Soviet bloc countries. I noticed Hungarian, Bulgarian, Russian and even Chinese labels on the various canned vegetables and fruits on display. With regard to the two last-named categories of foodstuffs, the prevalence of canned over fresh supplies was very conspicuous.

7

Berlin:
The Other Half

Now for a day-to-day, blow-by-blow account of my travels in the DDR and of the varied impressions I gathered in the course of this tour. Even as I started writing this book, in August, 1961, the border between East and West Berlin was shut tight by unilateral action of the East German authorities,in order to halt the ever swelling flow of refugees to the West. In a matter of weeks, the "Wall of Shame" was in place.

When I was in Berlin, the gates were still wide open. Having arrived at Tempelhof Airport, in the western half of the city, I crossed into the eastern sector in the simplest possible manner by buying a subway ticket and descending into the bowels of the free world at the Tempelhof Underground Station only to reemerge, a few minutes later, to the daylight of the Socialist Camp at Oranienburger Tor.

Although I had made a similar trip before — in 1958 — I still felt it to be a remarkable experience. Here, in the midst of a dark tunnel, I was crossing the Great Divide, the Iron Curtain, the demarcation line between two hostile worlds, without knowing exactly where the boundary ran. From a look at the subway map I could tell that it must have been somewhere underneath Friedrichstrasse, at the Zimmerstrasse intersection, between the stations of Kochstrasse — last stop in the Western sector — and Stadtmitte, the first in the eastern, or, according to the official lingo, "Democratic sector" of Berlin.

Outwardly, there appeared to be little change from one subway station to the next, the most noticeable perhaps being the fact that now a woman, instead of a man, was station manager, a first sign of the severe manpower shortage that is the most serious economic problem of the DDR. A glance at the newspaper and tobacco stands, however, instantly revealed the abrupt transition from one world to another. Instead of the fat, lively, frequently showy West German newspapers and magazines were the lean, doctrinaire and tedious products of Communist-controlled publishing houses; instead of the rich assortment of cigarettes and cigars of West German manufacture, a handful of standardized products of doubtful quality.

Not knowing exactly where the East German "Federation of Journalists," which had invited me, had their headquarters on Friedrichstrasse, one of the longest streets in Berlin, I got off at the wrong station and had to trudge back quite a distance, in driving rain, suitcase in hand.

My first impression of East Berlin, as I walked back to Friedrichstrasse Station was that motor traffic had greatly increased since I last had visited these parts in 1958. Later, on the autobahn to Leipzig and Dresden and on roads throughout the country this impression was confirmed. There are far more automobiles, both passenger cars and trucks, on the road these days than there were three years ago; the number of motorcycles and "mopeds" (motor-driven bicycle) has grown even more impressively.

The progress of motoring also was brought home to me in another, unexpected fashion. Checking my records on East Germany before starting out in this trip, I had come across an item in a leading West German newspaper that decried the small

number of driving schools in East Berlin, compared to the many
to be found in the western part of the city (the figures were 3
to 179, if I remember right). Yet at the first intersection, the loud
imprecations of an old man who had almost been knocked down
by a car turning into a side street aroused me to the realization
that the vehicle now heading for me was indeed one of those
public menaces — a driving-school car, jampacked with learn-
ers. After that experience I couldn't help wondering whether
they really were as scarce in East Berlin as that paper said . . .

A quarter mile or so further down the street, past the Spree
River bridge, a stately new building came into view. Windows
and showcases displaying books, magazines and pictures led
me to believe this must be the "Haus der Presse" (Press Center)
I was looking for. I walked in and inquired at the reception desk
for the person I was supposed to get in touch with on arrival.
The man at the desk looked up in astonishment; he spoke German haltingly, with an accent. Then I realized that I was in
the wrong place. This was not the Press Center; it was the
"House of Polish Culture" — one of several such cultural missions from other Soviet Bloc countries to be found in East
Berlin.

The Press Center, however, was almost next door. A much
smaller building, and rather unassuming. In fact, it turned out
to be little more than a clubhouse operated by the Federation
of Journalists; a pleasant enough place, though, with comfortable reading rooms, conference halls and a good restaurant.

I was received very hospitably, even cordially. The friendly
personal relations that were established the first day between
the secretary of the organization, Herr Strohbusch, his assistants
and myself endured throughout my stay in the country, in spite
of the animated, at times heated debates that were to take place
not only in Berlin but also with members of the local chapters
of the Federation in Leipzig and Karl-Marx-Stadt. In these ver-

bal bouts, some of which lasted until the wee hours of the morning, all current German as well as international problems were thrashed out. While I frequently had to concede I was impressed by this or that I had seen in the DDR, I never failed to emphasize that the absence of true democracy, the lack of political freedom, and the censorship of all news and opinion laid an unbridgeable abyss between the host country and my accustomed way of life.

Nowhere, I noticed, did my American citizenship give rise to any resentment per se. Rather, it used to arouse considerable curiosity, and I was frequently plied with questions about the U.S.A. The fact that I was born in Germany and spoke the language fluently helped, of course, facilitate the exchange of views. Our frank debates never led to ruffled feelings or left a bad taste in the mouth. And, I must say, I met with much less official reticence than I had expected. I was given every facility to see what I wanted to see, my liberty of movement was not restricted, I was provided with all the information and documentation I asked for and came away satisfied that I had accomplished my purpose — to get a comprehensive first-hand view of the country, its people, its accomplishments and its shortcomings. From the first day to the last, my hosts were courteous, cooperative and cordial. I am sincerely grateful for their assistance.

For the duration of my stay, an official limousine (a black "Tatra 603"), a driver and a guide selected from the membership of the Federation were put at my disposal. Both were pleasant, helpful and unobtrusive companions. It was not, therefore, a "conducted tour", in the sense that I was watched every minute and could not go out on my own. While I have little doubt that I was discreetly kept under observation (elsewhere the same thing usually happens), I was quite free in my movements. More then once my guide, Herr Herms (an editor of the official foreign policy review *Aussenpolitik*) told me, "Why don't you go out a bit on your own and look around for yourself?" I did.

The first two days of my sojourn in the DDR were devoted to a tour of East Berlin, a sprawling city in its own right. Being a reporter rather than a tourist, I was not much interested in sightseeing as such. Nevertheless, I welcomed the opportunity to drive through all parts of the city and get a good view of residential districts, factories and office buildings, administrative headquarters, public buildings, parks and monuments and so forth.

In the center of East Berlin the havoc created by the last war has not yet been wiped out completely. There are still many vacant lots, some of which have not even been cleared of the ruins and rubble. Here and there, rows of gutted buildings line silent streets that look almost deserted. True, there are also many signs of new constructions, but on the whole the central districts, which were destroyed most thoroughly, are lagging far behind the outlying sections and suburban areas where new blocks of apartment houses and new public buildings are everywhere going up.

This, I was informed, is the result of a policy decision. Because of the desperate housing shortage (which incidentally is not much worse than in West Germany, where moderately-priced apartments and houses are still in short supply in spite of an "overheated building boom") the government in the past few years has concentrated its reconstruction efforts on the outer sections of the city. There, standardized housing could be more quickly erected; the rebuilding of the center along "Socialist" lines would take more thorough planning and presents many complex problems. A start has been made, though, and reconstruction of the central districts is expected to be completed by 1965.

In new construction, the trend is toward ever increasing use of prefabricated sections and the perfection of standard techniques. Whereas the first apartment houses and stores on East Berlin's "show boulevard", Stalinallee,* were elaborately ornate in what is known as "Zuckerbäckerstil", a kind of architectural cheesecake copied from the Russians, the blocks of apartment houses now being built feature extreme simplicity and a total absence of decorative detail. Yet, despite their severe lines and the coarse building material — mostly concrete — used, the crisscross rows of housing blocks recently built or in the process of construction in many parts of East Berlin and elsewhere do not look ugly. They are far from being "barracks", as they are sometimes referred to in the West German press, and they are usually set in satisfactorily pleasant surroundings, complete with lawns, playgrounds and parking lots.

In the course of a visit to an impressive "Bauausstellung" (Building Exhibition) on Stalinallee, city architect Helmut Hennig took pains to explain to me what was being built and how.

In an attempt to provide a maximum of new dwellings in the shortest possible time, at the lowest possible cost and, especially, at the greatest possible saving of precious man-hours, new techniques of standardization were being constantly developed. Since about 1958 the traditional, individualistic, brick-by-brick building method has been replaced first by the "Grossblockbauweise" in which large prefabricated blocks of concrete were piled upon each other by powerful cranes; still more recently, the "Grossplattenbauweise" has come into fairly general use. This means that huge slabs of concrete, each weighing several

---

*As a result of the new "De-stalinization" drive launched by Khrushchev late in 1961, the "Stalinallee" recently has been renamed "Karl Marx Allee." At the same time, the town of Stalinstadt (cf. Chapter 10) became "Eisenhüttenstadt."

tons, are lifted up, hooked to each other and then welded together. In this manner, an entire wall of a fair-sized room can
be put into place in one operation. For outside walls, the slabs
have built-in windows. According to the figures supplied by
Herr Hennig, new apartments now are being completed in
about one-third of the time previously required. Whereas, for
example, a standard apartment of 55 square meters living
space previously took 2300 man-hours to build, the same apartment now can be built in 760 hours.*

However — this information was not exactly volunteered, but
developed through "cross-examination" — this high degree of industrialization solves only half of the problem, if indeed it solves
that much. For, what it does is merely to speed the outer shell of
a new apartment building. But then comes the hitch — there usually is a hitch somewhere in the best-laid plans of mice, men and
Communist perfectionists — and it's a big one.

In order to turn this rapidly-thrown-together shell of building
into a place where human beings can live decently, the help of
many craftsmen — painters, plumbers, electricians and so forth
— is needed. In such trades, there are manpower shortages even
in West Germany and other Western countries where the skilled
craftsman is treated like a king. In the DDR, where many of
these artisans have been pressed into cooperatives controlled by
the State and the Party, with the loss of incentive and personal
enterprise that usually results from this operation, the shortage
is catastrophic. Until most recently, it was further aggravated
by the lure of West Berlin, where a skilled craftsman, even one

---

*One of the reasons why the Communist authorities, in August, 1961,
were able to throw up the Berlin inter-city wall with such amazing
speed and precision was precisely the availability for immediate use — a
very different one from that originally planned — of a large supply of
such concrete blocks and slabs.

resident in the eastern sector of the city, could earn up to four times the amount of money he could make at home, due to the fact that one West mark is worth about four-and-a-half East marks on the free exchange.

In this connection, a word should be said about another serious problem the government of the DDR has been faced with, at least as long as the free flow of people across the dividing line in Berlin prevailed. If the East German authorities complained that the chronic, or periodically recurring shortages of certain foodstuffs, other consumer goods and services were partly caused by West Berliners who "drained away" what rightly belonged to the inhabitants of the eastern sector, this is not propaganda, but fact.

Indeed, the truth of this assertion is self-evident, human nature being what it is. For a long time, West Berliners were taking advantage of the fact that their money's buying power increased fourfold or more the moment they stepped across the demarcation line to go shopping on the other side. East German butter tasted just as good as West German butter; in East Berlin restaurants, meals compared in quantity, quality and price with those of West Berlin, as I have noted before; an East Berlin haircut would do just as well as one obtained, at about four times the price in West Berlin; and a pair of shoes bought in East Berlin, while it probably would not last quite as long as one acquired in the Western sectors, would still give plenty of mileage at low cost to the buyer from West Berlin.

Needless to say, the East German authorities took steps long ago to correct this situation. The importation of East marks bought cheaply in the West has been unlawful for many years while the official rate of exchange remained pegged to an unrealistic 1:1. And a spate of ordinances issued by the East Berlin City Council gradually reduced the area of unrestricted shopping to the point where in the end one couldn't buy a box of matches, let alone a pack of cigarettes or any object of real value without proving to the satisfaction of the seller (and to the cop who stands behind him invisibly) that he was a citizen of the DDR. Nor could one eat in a restaurant, have a cup of coffee or tea in a café, get a haircut or obtain any other valuable service without producing his identity card (or, for a foreigner, his passport with a valid DDR-visa stamped into it). If the passport or identity card showed the holder to be a resident of West Berlin or West Germany, he was required to pay for all goods bought, or services obtained, in West marks.

Yet, in spite of all official restrictions, the drain continued. A big city like Berlin, where almost everyone has relatives, acquaintances or good friends on the other side and where two great transportation networks (the U-Bahn or Subway and the S-Bahn or City Railroad) used to cross the East-West demarcation line not just once, but in cases twice, on one trip from terminal to terminal, was a place full of loopholes. And the Berliners are known to be "helle" or canny, a people conditioned by long adversity to all the tricks for making the best of a bad situation.

And so, for all the bans and checks devised by the East German regime, West Berlin housewives went on stocking their refrigerators with butter, eggs and meat cheaply bought from East German sources; men, women and children of West Berlin kept wearing clothes fashioned from textiles acquired in the East at a 75% discount; and, occasionally, West Berliners would gorge themselves and drink to their hearts' content in an East Berlin luxury restaurant at the bargain rate of the century.

This constant drain, along with the powerful temptation for East Berlin craftsmen to practice their trade in the western half of the city, undoubtedly has harmed the East German economy. It has been a factor (not the only one, of course) in the depletion of East German stocks of foodstuffs and consumer goods and has contributed to the fact that many a new apartment building, erected in record time, remained for months an empty shell because no painters, plumbers and electricians were available to finish the job.

Realization of this abnormal state of affairs will help one understand the harsh measures the East German Government adopted in mid-August 1961 to close the gap and to keep at home the goods produced on its territory as well as the people living under its rule, whether they liked it or not. Even so, however, the East German Government certainly had no right to change the four-power-status of Berlin unilaterally, as it did.

8

Leipzig
Between Fairs

"I wish you had come here at Fair time, sir," the leader of the local reception committee sighed, "there is so much more going on then."

I thanked the gentleman for his solicitude for my entertainment and assured him I would have loved to see the Fair (a white lie — trade fairs bore me), but added I had reasons to be quite happy to see Leipzig between fairs (one is held in the spring, the other in the fall of each year).

While I did not elaborate on what these reasons were, I suppose my host could guess, for he smiled. When the Fair is on, Leipzig attracts large crowds of visitors, many of them from abroad. Along with the businessmen, scores of reporters then descend on the city, which naturally uses the occasion to primp and preen itself (any city would).

These efforts at embellishment do not, as a rule, escape the attention of argus-eyed foreign and West German journalists determined not to be taken in by false pretenses. Their comments, in the press of their home countries, then usually run along these lines: "Sure, while the Fair is on, Leipzig is a pretty good place to live in. Then you can get everything you want. The bare shelves in the government-operated stores suddenly fill up as if by magic; the awful food in the restaurants becomes eatable; they even put a dash of the real thing into the sickening ersatz brew they call coffee (of all the bad cups of coffee served throughout Germany, the Saxons traditionally have a reputation for making the worst). But, just wait for the foreign visitors to leave. The moment they're gone, everything goes back to its normal state of want and disrepair."

I have read this kind of story about the Leipzig Fair many times, and I was anxious, therefore, to check on its content of truth — which I found to be low. Leipzig without Fair looked pretty good to me, although, as a matter of fact, I have always been a little prejudiced against this city, which I had known in my early youth. I don't quite know myself why I never liked Leipzig. Was it the huge, sombre railroad station, an architectural eyesore conceived by megalomaniac empire-builders, that repelled me? The absence of a great river, or other major waterway (an asset to every city)? The hectic commercialism of a big business metropolis? Or the lack of scenic surroundings? Any and all of these factors might have influenced my feelings.

On the other hand, there always was something about Leipzig that must needs appeal to one who makes his living by writing. Of all German cities, Leipzig has traditionally been the "Buchstadt" (Book Town) par excellence: the seat of countless publishing firms; the center of the printing trade; a city teeming with book stores; and the home of the greatest German library. In going to Leipzig, therefore, I was looking forward particularly to a tour of "Book Town" and to talks with book publishers, book sellers and librarians. Before I set down my impressions on this subject, first a word about the trip itself.

Leipzig, with a population of 592,821 (as of January 1, 1960), is the second-largest city of the DDR, after the capital,

East Berlin (pop.: 1,082,349). It is the largest of "the Republic", as the territory outside of Berlin is called in the peculiar lingo of the DDR.

Linked to the capital by a fine stretch of autobahn (generally speaking the East German autobahn is in much better condition than its West German counterpart, due, of course, to the fact that there is far less traffic), Leipzig nevertheless is not as easily accessible as it looks on a map. The traveler starting out from East Berlin is forced to make a considerable detour to get there, because the direct autobahn route from Berlin to Leipzig crosses the Western sectors. There is, however, another autobahn stretch that skirts Berlin and links up with the one leading to Leipzig at a point below Potsdam. Several roads lead from East Berlin to this all-DDR autobahn, but the traveler has to make up his mind about which one to choose before he starts out in his trip. For his papers are stamped valid for only one checkpoint, and if he changes his itinerary en route he is liable to arrive at a control station where he will not be allowed to pass.

Before the actual experience, I had no idea how much red tape is involved in touring the DDR. Indeed, I can think of no other instance where people traveling from the capital of a country to the provinces, or states, or vice-versa, are checked, in peacetime, for passports and visas. Yet such is the practice in the DDR. All exits from East Berlin into "the Republic" lead to checkpoints which are heavily guarded by People's Police and border guards. In order to get through, you have to have not only a valid passport and a valid visa, but also a dated permit to pass through this particular checkpoint!

In my case, this caused a bit of trouble because my hosts had mapped out an extensive travel program only to discover at the last minute that a given hotel was booked full and there were no alternative accommodations to be had in that particular city. As a result, the whole tour had to be rerouted and a new itinerary was picked. But my passport had already been stamped for a different checkpoint from the one we now were going to pass through! When our driver realized this (we were already on our way) he paled and rushed off to the proper authorities to have the entry in my passport changed at the last minute.

The trip from Berlin to Leipzig was uneventful, but a bit tiresome. Autobahn "raststätten" (i.e. restaurants with lounges, rest rooms, and in some cases motels which, in West Germany, by their number and variety pleasantly break up the monotony of speedway traveling) still are few and far between in the DDR. I noticed, though, that one or two new ones had been built along stretches I had driven through in 1958.

On the other hand, there is a marked increase in the number of filling stations, not only along the autobahn, but also on other roads and city streets. The service is better, too, than it used to be. Only one brand of gasoline ("Minol") is on sale, in two qualities. Both are horribly expensive, the cheaper one costing 140 pfennigs, the other 150 pfennigs per liter, as compared to an average price of 56 pfennigs for ordinary and 63 pfennigs for "super" gasoline in West Germany. (One mark— 100 pfennigs—U.S. $.25.)

To come back to Leipzig, I found a bustling city, with many attractive and generally well-stocked stores and fine restaurants. (In contrast to East Berlin, one doesn't need a passport or identity card in any city or town of "the Republic" in order to buy things in a store or get service in a restaurant or café, the reason being that it isn't nearly so easy outside Berlin to smuggle in East marks bought in the West.)

I ate some of my meals at my hotel, the "Astoria", others at famed "Auerbachs Keller", an historic eating place where Goethe used to dine and wine. In both restaurants the food was excellent and, on the average, not more expensive than it would be in a comparable place and city of West Germany.

At the "Astoria", I did a disgraceful thing,which I can only hope to have excused in the interest of documentation: I swiped the menu (state property, if you please!). I did the same thing again at the "Ratskeller" in the town of Meissen, a lower-class establishment where the food, however, was almost as good as in the high-class Leipzig restaurants. I'm holding these two exhibits ready for inspection by any skeptic who doubts that one can eat well, at a reasonable price, in the DDR. I can vouch for the fact that the items listed on the menu actually were available at the time and also that helpings, as a rule, were at least as generous as they are in West Germany.

In deference to my special interests and in view of the short time available, sightseeing in Leipzig again was held down to a minimum. A glimpse of the venerable Town Hall; a brief stop at the colossal monument commemorating the "Battle of Nations"; a leisurely stroll through the picturesque streets and squares of the old city; and a performance at the brand-new Opera House — about which more will be said further on — that was about all that could be crowded into a program preempted by several visits to "Book Town", the University and a newspaper plant. My hosts were slightly miffed because I would not even include a glance at two of Leipzig's most famous landmarks, one old, the Fair Grounds (what good are they to the visitor when empty?); the other new, the "German Academy of Physical Culture and Sports", which boasts the largest and most modern stadium in Germany.

The Central Library

Founded in 1912 on the initiative of the German Booksellers' Association, the "Deutsche Bücherei" at Leipzig used to be the National Library of Germany. It still is in some measure, although its usefulness has been greatly impaired by the division of Germany and especially by the fact that it is now under the control of a regime that does not respect the freedom of expression.

Physically, the Library, whose main building (erected in 1914-16) faces "Deutscher Platz", is still expanding. It has long since outgrown the space originally available. A wing added in 1936 proved insufficient to cope with the rising flood of new acquisitions which now average 50,000 "bibliographic units" annually. Since March 25, 1959, a vast enlargement program has been under way. In the first stage, another new wing is to be built; it is to be completed by October 1962 when the Library will celebrate its 50th anniversary (at present, construction has reached approximately the half-way mark). Later, several new floors are to be added to the wing built in 1936. A total of 5,000,000 marks has been allocated for these extensions and improvements.

According to the most recent figures supplied to me by the press offices of the Library, the "Deutsche Bücherei," at the end of 1960, possessed 2,824,708 volumes. The four reading rooms, with a present capacity of about 500 seats, were used, in 1960, by 184,033 readers.

A tour of these reading rooms showed that there were few empty seats. Most of the readers appeared to be students. I noted that the Periodicals Room was the least crowded. One reason may be that the literary fare offered there is rather meager. Among the roughly 3,000 journals and magazines on display, there were *none* from West Germany, or any other German-speaking country other than the DDR, except for purely scientific or scholarly publications. General magazines, political journals, economic reviews, etc., from outside the DDR were conspicuously absent.

In the reference department, too, the heavy hand of political censorship was apparent. I had heard before that librarians in the DDR made a practice of secluding in so-called "Sperrbibliotheken" (blocked library sections) all West German, and generally all Western, books considered hostile to the Ulbricht regime or to its Soviet sponsors and associates. Only persons doing scholarly research and considered politically reliable, or those serving Communist propaganda purposes, were supposed to have access to these closed sections, humorously referred to as "Giftschränke" or poison cabinets.

I asked the library official who accompanied us on our tour whether this information was correct. Rather to my surprise, he made no attempt to deny it. Indeed, he showed me the special catalogue in which these books were listed under various classifications, the most severe being "Hetzschriften" or hate literature. When I jokingly inquired whether any of my own books had been banished to the "poison cabinet", he looked up my name in the author catalogue and showed me the entries. All four of my German-language books published since 1956 were listed and though some of them bore cryptic annotations, it appeared none of them had been put on the index, at any rate not its section of "untouchables".

From the Library, we went to the headquarters of the "Börsenverein deutscher Buchhändler" or German Booksellers' Association, which continues to do business, in both parts of divided Germany, under the same name but under altogether different colors. It is in fact an organization of book publishers, rather than booksellers. One of its main functions nowadays is to publish the trade organ *Börsenblatt* (roughly equivalent to *Publishers' Weekly*) which, curiously enough, also comes out under the same name, but in totally different editions, in the two rival German "book towns" Frankfurt-on-Main and Leipzig. One lists only the books published in the Federal Republic; the other those published in the DDR. Seldom, if ever, do they take any notice of each other, or cross lines.

At the "Börsenverein" — twice a misnomer in the case of the Leipzig outfit, for "Börse" means Bourse or Exchange and

"Verein" means association — I obtained the latest figures concerning public ownership in the book trade. I was told that there are now 65 so-called "volkseigene Betriebe" (VEB's) or state-enterprises in the publishing field, as compared to 33 private publishers still in business. Even in the last-named category, however, the State usually has a finger in the pie and all publishing firms, of course, are under the thumb of rigorous censorship.

In the field of bookselling, the ratio is more favorable to private enterprise. If the figures I was given are correct, there are in the DDR at present 1,960 privately operated bookstores, against 675 so-called "Volksbuchhandlungen" or state-owned ones.

In Leipzig, I also visited various departments of the famous old university, now renamed "Karl-Marx-Universität", and I had a very interesting talk with Professor Hans Teubner, editor of "Leipziger Volkszeitung", one of the leading newspapers of the DDR. What I learned in the course of these visits and conversations, will be related in the special chapters on East German education and journalism to be found below.

9

Dresden Rises
From the Ashes

Among the major cities of the DDR, Dresden, the old capital of Saxony, has the distinction of possessing the most attractive and modern, as well as the best-stocked stores; the finest, in a word, I saw anywhere in the course of my trip, which took me to all parts of the country, except Thuringia and the Magdeburg-Halle area in the west. (The only reason why this portion of the country was not included in the itinerary was lack of time. It was myself, not my hosts, who had set ten days as the outside limit of my stay in the DDR; this limitation was made necessary by other commitments.)

Not only the experience of Dresden, but also what I saw in Leipzig, Karl-Marx-Stadt, Rostock and elsewhere, convinced me that it is definitely not true that East Berlin — which is easily accessible to foreigners, who invariably find it drab by comparison with West Berlin — represents the "show-case" of the DDR. The implication of this assertion is, of course, that, since East Berlin looks so shabby to Westerners, conditions elsewhere in the "zone" must be unbelievably bad and dreary.

Actually, just the opposite is true. In half a dozen cities, but especially at Dresden (population: nearly 500,000), there are

stores, restaurants, cafés and other establishments far superior
to what you would find in East Berlin. Far from being the show
case, East Berlin rather is the Cinderella of East German
cities. Why? I suppose the fundamental reason is that the Ulbricht regime does not discount the possibility it may have to
relinquish its control of East Berlin, or part of it, anyway, in
the interest of a peaceful settlement of the Berlin problem
that would reunite the divided city under a new, internation-
ally guaranteed statute. In any event, the East German planners seem to feel it is safer for them to invest in the reconstruction of other cities.

Dresden's new shopping district, which centers on bustling
Thälmannstrasse, covers a block of streets in the neighborhood
of the old business center where once some of Germany's greatest department stores stood and where to this day ruins and
heaps of rubble meet the eye. This whole area was virtually
razed on Dresden's Doomsday, February 13-14, 1945, when
one of the heaviest air raids of the war all but completely
devastated the center of what had been one of Germany's most
beautiful cities, a city which prided itself on being a "Flor-
ence-on-the-Elbe". (The American visitor is invariably told,
in tones of self-righteous indignation, that Dresden was destroyed by a wanton "terror raid" the U.S. Forces staged for the
sole purpose of depriving the Red Army, which then was approaching the city, of what would have been one of its finest
prizes.)

While many of Dresden's historic monuments have been rebuilt — in particular, restoration of the world-famous Zwin-
ger, one of Europe's most beautiful baroque buildings, is nearly completed — large sections of the former business center
and adjoining residential areas still lie waste. For, in Dresden, as in East Berlin and in other cities, the reconstruction
policy of the powers-that-be has been first to create new suburban settlements, in order to take the worst sting out of the

house shortage as quickly as possible, and then gradually to progress from the outlying districts towards the center, where the problems of rebuilding are most complex.

In the case of Dresden, the key problem is how to harmonize the "Socialist" construction goals with the traditional charm of a city which owes most of its picturesque beauty to royal fancy. However, as in East Berlin, wholesale reconstruction of the central districts now is well under way and is expected to be completed in the main by 1965.

In the economic scheme of things, Dresden now again ranks as one of the principal industrial cities of Eastern Germany. Machine-building and heavy engineering as well as the production of radio and television sets, cameras, motion picture equipment and photographic supplies figure among the chief local industries.

Dresden, or more exactly the village of Rossendorf, some six miles away from the city, has been since 1955 a major center of atomic research and development, a field in which the East Germans claim to be well ahead of their competitors in the Federal Republic. A cyclotron of 25 million electrovolts has been in operation since August 1, 1958, and a betatron was added on January 15, 1959.

Until a few months ago, Dresden was also an aircraft manufacturing center where four-engined jet planes "BB 152" were being built. In the spring of 1961, however, the entire aviation industry of the DDR was suddenly scrapped without plausible explanation, and the Dresden plant was converted to other industrial purposes. This move apparently was prompted by a Kremlin policy decision that reserved the manufacture of aircraft for the entire Soviet Bloc to Russian industry alone.

Dresden plays an important part in education and cultural activities, too. The country's leading Institute of Technology, a College of Transportation and other specialized schools are located there. Dresden also prides itself on being again what it used to be in the old days — one of Germany's leading cities of art. Many famous art collections and museums (including, as a rarity, a "Museum of Hygiene") grace the old city which was, in its heyday, the capital of an important kingdom but now ranks more modestly as administrative center of the "District of Dresden", one of fourteen in the country.

10

Red Model City:
Stalinstadt*

"The sausages we make here every month", my cicerone proud-
ly proclaimed, pointing to the big plant labeled "Fleishkom-
binat" (meat combine), "laid end to end would reach from
this city to Schwedt" (one of the next destinations on my itinerary, some 93 miles away).

Taking my polite exclamation for an expression of real interest in the matter, my guide went off on more butchery statistics: "In our meat combine, every 39.6 seconds a slaughtered
pig comes off the conveyor belt."

I don't doubt it. The East Germans are the world's cham-
pion sausage eaters. They beat in this field even their country-
men in the Federal Republic, which is saying a lot. Whenever a local or seasonal meat shortage occurs in the DDR, and
butcher shops are bare of choice cuts, you'll still find the ubiquitous fat, juicy Bockwurst hanging from the ceiling or a
rack. And the no less ubiquitous Bockwurst stands never seem
to run out of supplies. Thanks, among others, to that brand-
new, model slaughter-house at Stalinstadt where every 39 sec-

---

*See footnote, p. 71.

onds a live pig is put on a rolling line and comes out as sausage meat at the other end.

But, I had not come to Stalinstadt, a city so far stubbornly ignored by the world's mapmakers, but very much in existence, to talk sausages or to inspect meat combines. Stalinstadt possesses other and more substantial titles to fame, and my time was limited.

For one thing, Stalinstadt is the most important metallurgical center in the DDR. It would be simpler, of course, to say it is the country's biggest "steel city", but it would also be inaccurate. For Stalinstadt, while making more than a million tons of pig iron yearly, still has to produce its first ton of steel. One might call it an "iron city",* therefore, it definitely is not a "steel city" the way Pittsburgh or Essen are.

This is only the first of Stalinstadt's many peculiarities. Normally, where iron is made, steel is also produced and rolled. Not here. While the iron works are at Stalinstadt (and at Maximilianshütte of Unterwellenborn, where an older and smaller plant of this kind exists), the steel works are to be found elsewhere (at Brandenburg, Henningsdorf, Riesa, Gröditz, etc.). Not until 1965, at the earliest, will Stalinstadt have a steel mill, too.

Even more unusual is the location of East Germany's "iron city". For, in the normal course of things, an iron and steel industry develops in a region rich in either iron ore or coal deposits or both. The soil, however, on which Stalinstadt was built, holds no mineral riches whatsoever. It is part of the Mark Brandenburg "sandbox", as the flat, sparsely wooded and generally barren land southeast of Berlin is popularly called. In fact, this is the sandiest stretch of them all, for here, in the wide river valley between Guben and Frankfurt-on-

---

* "Eisenhüttenstadt", the town's official new name, means "Iron Mines City."

the Oder, the mighty stream, over the centuries, has deposited huge quantities of sand and silt it carries along in flood.

The pig iron that Stalinstadt's six mighty blast furnaces now produce at a rate of about 1.2 million tons a year is made from *Soviet* iron ore and *Polish* coke. Other minerals required in the process, especially large quantities of manganese, are also imported from the Soviet Union. The only element of importance in the production process that is locally available is lime — and even that has to be hauled to Stalinstadt over a long distance, for it comes from the Hartz Mountains on the western border of the DDR.

What considerations, then, led to the decision, made in the summer of 1950, to build from scratch an iron and (in the future) steel city of large proportions in an area that had nothing to offer but sand and pinewoods? From what I gathered in talks with Stalinstadt officials and technicians, the choice of this particular location — about 2 1/2 miles west of the old town of Fürstenberg on the Oder — was dictated mainly by two reasons.

In the first place, two important waterways are conveniently near for shipping raw materials and finished products: the Oder, and the Oder-Spree-Canal built in 1891 to link the confluence area of the Oder and Neisse rivers with the far-flung system of waterways that surrounds Berlin. Also, a major railroad line connects nearby Fürstenberg — now the smaller of the two twin cities — with the chief town and administrative capital of the district, Frankfurt-on-the-Oder. Thus, the experts reckoned, the huge amounts of iron ore to be imported from the Soviet Union (1.8 million tons in 1959) and of coke to be imported from Poland (1.6 million tons in 1959) could be shipped to Stalinstadt more economically than to any other site that was then being considered.

There was, however, another and perhaps dominant consideration which one might call strategic were it not that it so strangely runs counter to all traditional concepts of strategic planning. For Stalinstadt, destined to become an economic nerve center of first-rate importance, is only about three miles distant from the Polish border. (Much the same holds good of another vitally important undertaking, the big oil refinery of Schwedt which will be discussed in Chapter 12.) Thus the Poles could quickly strike crippling blows at the DDR, if ever there developed an armed conflict between the two countries. This contingency, though, appears to have been ruled out by the Kremlin which of course has had the last say in the matter, and which decided, therefore, that the two strategically important ventures should be placed as far away as possible from the scope of West German military might.

Stalinstadt owes its very existence to the division of Germany into mutually hostile halves after the last war. For, as a result of this split, the Soviet Zone and later the "German Democratic Republic" that sprang from it, found itself cut off from the immense industrial potential of the Ruhr. Indeed, in 1945, the eastern zone's iron-making capacity was only 200,000 tons annually, or about 1.7% of the German total. On the other hand, about 50% of Germany's textile and machine tool building industries had been allotted to the Soviet zone — a glaring discrepancy between industrial capacity and available supplies of basic raw materials.

Hence the decision, first announced at the Socialist Unity Party's third national convention, on July 21, 1950, to erect a large new ironworks for smelting imported ore was economically sound. (East Germany mines some iron ore, but it is of inferior quality.) And so the "Eisenhüttenkombinat" (iron-smelting combine) *J. W. Stalin*, named by the arch-Stalinist Walter Ulbricht after his boss and idol, was born.

Even before that date, groups of surveyors had been sent to the Fürstenberg area to stake off a suitable tract of land. This soon was cleared in a hurry of the pine trees and shrubs native to the region.On August 18, 1950, ground was formally broken and leveling began with the help of earth-moving equipment supplied by the Soviet Union. By January 1, 1951, work had progressed to the point where the foundation of the first blast furnace could be laid; it was put in service on September 19, 1951. Three more blast furnaces went into operation in the course of 1952; a fifth was added on October 31, 1953 and the sixth was completed in August, 1954.

However, everything did not go as smoothly as planned. A major difficulty from the start was the shortage of trained workers and generally the lack of know-how. The large majority of the men and women who now make up the combine's labor force had been small trades-people, farmhands or drifters rather than ironworkers; many of them had never even seen a blast furnace before. Some were sent to the older "Maximilianshütte" for specialized training, but most of them learned their complex new jobs by trial and error, in hit-or-miss fashion. A source of many hitches in the beginning was failure to compose the layers of ore, lime and coke in exactly the right proportion. In 1952 so many kinks developed in the production process that a rescue team of Soviet metallurgists and engineers had to be sent from the Donbass (Donetz Basin) to straighten things out.

On at least two occasions — once, toward the end of 1951 when a tall steel frame toppled, and again in the winter 1952-53, when a special plant for thawing the chunks of iron ore frozen in transport was destroyed by fire — "saboteurs" were blamed for these mishaps. A grisly incident occurred early in the process of excavation when a mass grave containing the bodies of more than 4,000 prisoners slain by the Nazis — most of the victims were Russians — was uncovered. In their honor, a handsome, 55 foot high monument was set up on the site that later was to become one of Stalinstadt's principal squares, called "Place of German-Soviet Amity".

Despite numerous setbacks and repeated failures to fulfil five-year-plan targets, the Combine, in due course, became the country's principal supplier of pig iron. As more and more blast furnaces went into operation, output increased from 3,539 tons of pig iron in 1951 to 264,446 in 1952; 568,251 in 1953; 730,182 in 1954; 912,281 in 1955; 925,191 in 1956; 976,250 in 1957; 1,076,254 in 1958; and 1,121,406 in 1959. By comparison, the total output of pig iron in the DDR was 1,517,000 tons in 1955; 1,775,000 in 1958; and 1,898,000 in 1959. Thus, the Combine at present accounts for about two-thirds of total production. A large number of by-products are also turned out by the Combine. One of them is a gas residue used to feed the turbines of a big power plant, said to be capable of delivering 600 million kilowatt-hours a year.

Construction costs, up to and including 1959, totaled 451 million East marks. An even larger sum will be invested in the erection of a fully mechanized and to the largest possible extent automatized steel mill and rolling plant due to go into production toward the end of 1965, along with other enlargements and improvements foreseen by the current economic plan. The present work force of 5,758 (23.6% women) is to be doubled eventually.

Along with, and close to, the industrial combine that gave it its name, a brand-new city with a present population of 24,000 was built from scratch according to a precise blueprint drawn by Communist planners. It was this Red Model City, which prides itself on being "the first Socialist town of Germany," rather than the ironworks, I had come to study at close quarters.

I came away with mixed feelings. In many ways, Stalinstadt is very impressive. Nowhere else in the DDR (except perhaps at Dresden) have I seen more attractive and well-built apartment houses, or stores as trim, as well-stocked and inviting as those of Stalinstadt. Streets and squares are neatly cut, clean and polished. Concentric blocks of apartment buildings, built in varying styles, from the most sternly functionalist to tastefully decorative, are set apart by well-kept lawns and tidy patches of greenery. No dark alleys or forbidding backyards anywhere.

In the latest-built of these settlements or "complexes of dwellings" (*Wohnkomplexe*), as they are called, great care has been taken to separate pedestrians and motor traffic as far as possible. For instance, special paths connect all buildings in the complex with the communal facilities and institutions belonging thereto without crossing a street. Thus, housewives and children, in particular, are sheltered from traffic hazards more than is ordinarily the case in a city.

Along the *Magistrale* or Main Street (its official name is Leninallee), three miniature skyscrapers, each ten stories high (which is pretty tall by European standards) tower above the surrounding blocks of stores and dwellings. A large department store, with a pleasant café on the top floor, also attracts attention from afar. Elsewhere in the city, I noticed a combined restaurant and café, complete with a spacious dance floor and four-man band, called "Aktivist", which is one of the swankiest establishments of this kind in the DDR; I doubt you'd find anything to match it in a West German industrial city of comparable size.

In the center of Stalinstadt, there is a stately, stylishly decorated and technically well-equipped motion picture theatre named after the dramatist Friedrich Wolf, where also stage shows are produced. Another even larger theater is to be built on Central Square ("Platz der Republik") where also a tall "House of Culture and Science" and other public buildings are to rise before 1965. In a charming pine grove, on the outskirts of town, one of the most beautiful open-air theaters I have seen anywhere has recently been inaugurated; it can accommodate 3,000 spectators.

I was also very favorably impressed by a visit to the "Ledi-genwohnheim" or Bachelors' Home on Maxim-Gorki-Strasse. There, unmarried young men and women can rent comfortably furnished one-room apartments with kitchenettes and (usually shared) bath for as low as 35 marks a month. (In West Germany, students and other impecunious bachelors pay 70 or 80 marks a month for rooms that offer neither the same comfort nor the same degree of privacy.)

Proudest feature of Stalinstadt, however, are its many schools which — in appearance and organization, anyway — are model institutions, with bright, airy classrooms and ample facilities for technical training, sports and recreation. I visited one of four "polytechnical high schools", a new type of ten-grade school attended by all children, and must say it measures up to the finest I have seen anywhere in Europe or in the United States. The school is flanked on one side by a kindergarten and on the other by a nursery. In all, some 2,500 small children are cared for in the city's nurseries and kindergartens of which there is one each in every "Wohnkomplex".

The city's health services, in which 1,100 people, i.e. almost one out of every twenty inhabitants, are employed, must also be described as exemplary. Stalinstadt boasts one of the largest and most modern hospitals in the country which has facilities not only for the workers of the Combine and the inhabitants of the city but also for out-of-town patients. By contrast, there are no churches at all in this "first Socialist city of Germany", though I understand that some religious services are held in makeshift quarters.

Stalinstadt is the youngest city of the DDR in a double sense. Not only because its foundations were laid barely ten years ago, but also on account of its peculiar age structure. One third of the population is made up of children under 15; the rest are mainly young or middle-aged adults. There is a remarkable gap in the 15 to 20 age group, which has the advantage that there is no juvenile delinquency to speak of. There are virtually no old people living in the city. The average age of the city's population is an amazingly low 27.

Like all pioneer and frontier towns, Stalinstadt has long been beset by a marked surplus of males, but of late the distribution of sexes has become more evenly balanced.

Stalinstadt's claim to being the first Socialist city of Germany is derived mainly from the total absence of private property and enterprise. Everything except personal things belongs to the state, the city or one of the many cooperatives. In Stalinstadt, even hairdressers, tailors, cobblers, carpenters and other craftsmen, who elsewhere in the DDR as a rule still operate private businesses, are grouped together in "production cooperatives". These are neither butchers nor bakers (least of all candlestick-makers), their places having been taken by huge factories or "combines" which not only supply the city itself, but also the surrounding countryside.

All things considered, this outwardly attractive blueprint of a Communist society in action comes uncomfortably close to George Orwell's grim version of a well-planned, technically perfect, but also dehumanized beehive state living a strictly regimented and colorless existence under the watchful eye of Big Brother. As a portent of things to come, it is not appealing. Not to me, anyway.

11

The "Black Pump" Combine

"Smoking in bed, as well as all cooking, ironing etc. in this hotel room is strictly prohibited."

I was just about to take out my little camping stove with the intention of fixing myself an early morning cup of coffee, when my eye caught the warning notice attached to the inside of the wardrobe.

Better obey the law, I thought, especially in this country where they take a stern view of trifling with police regulations (the East German Fire Department, incidentally, forms an integral part of the *Volkspolizei* or People's Police). Besides, in this particular case, my innocent purpose might be misinterpreted if I was found guilty of creating a fire hazard. I might be looked upon as a would-be arsonist, a fiendish saboteur sent by the "class enemy" with orders to set fire to one of the most ambitious building projects currently under way in the DDR — the "Black Pump" Combine.

For the small, but spick-and-span hotel where I was staying nestles on the edge of the sprawling new industrial compound between the towns of Spremberg and Hoyerswerda in the District of Cottbus, a compound that is destined to become the largest chemical combine in the DDR. Already, inflammable materials abound here, so the warning put up by the Fire Department is fully justified. A person who falls asleep smoking in bed may easily set a hotel on fire — and flying sparks from this burning building then might be carried by the wind into the works area, setting off tremendous explosions.

Although it represents, even in its present unfinished state, an industrial undertaking of breathtaking size and scope, the Black Pump Combine is not yet marked on any large-scale map of the area I have seen. Not even on those put out by the official East German publishing house "VEB Landkartenverlag" Berlin. This is understandable, though, for the "Black Pump" is a far more recent venture than Stalinstadt, which has won recognition at least from Eastern mapmakers.

The Black Pump Combine represents a palpable embodiment of the East German Government's determination to make the most of the country's limited natural resources. Indeed, the DDR's potentialities of economic growth have been handicapped from the start by the fact that it has just about the weakest energy base of any highly industrialized state in Europe. Its oil and natural gas resources are practically nil; its output of hard coal (2,841,000 tons in 1959) is negligible by comparison to that of the Federal Republic; and its water power is limited.

What the DDR, by contrast, does possess in abundance is brown coal or lignite (1959 output: 215 million tons). Hence a key factor in economic planning is to derive from this plentiful and cheap fuel the greatest possible variety of chemical and industrial products.

In the past, most of the brown coal used as household or industrial fuel in the DDR was *raw* coal; this was a highly wasteful method of burning up the country's most precious energy source. Even by turning the raw brown coal into briquettes first, a great deal of energy can be saved. Maximum use, however, can be achieved by converting the brown coal into so-called "Edelenergieträger" i.e. refined energy sources such as high-temperature coke for blast furnaces and chemical industries; gas and electric power; and finally liquid derivatives such as phenol, tars and motor fuel.

To achieve this purpose on a large scale, the "Black Pump" Combine was devised and has been under construction since 1955. When completed in 1965 (if work continues to progress on schedule as has been the case so far), the Combine will be the world's largest plant for processing brown coal, with a daily throughput of 100,000 tons of raw coal. Its output of gas alone will exceed that of all the 180 gas-works presently in operation in the DDR put together.

"Black Pump" — the name has no symbolic connotation but is derived from that of an old roadside inn "Zur Schwarzen Pumpe" which still stands on the edge of the compound — is the biggest and costliest of all the ambitious industrial undertakings launched by the East German Government. It will require total investments of at least 2.5 billion east marks,* not counting an additional billion needed for the modernization and expansion of the brown coal mines in the vicinity.

The building site (as in the case of Stalinstadt it was obtained through clearing a large tract of pinewoods) is by far the largest in the DDR. While I could not obtain precise figures about its size, I was told that its dimensions exceeded those of the Mueggelsee, a fair-sized lake on the outskirts of East Berlin which measures about 7.5 square kilometers. In any event, the maze of smokestacks, cooling towers, factories, power plants, gas tanks, conveyor belts, railroad tracks and so forth I saw stretched for miles around, as far as the eye could encompass. From personal observation I would say that the Combine, at this stage, is about one-third completed. At

---

*About $650,000 at the official rate.

least one of three planned work units consisting each of one power plant, one briquette factory, one cokery and the installations for drying and preparing the raw brown coal, is in full operation. So far, however, only briquettes are made in quantity.

What prompted the choice of this particular location (about halfway between the towns of Spremberg and Hoyerswerda, but a little closer to the first-named) as building site for the mammoth undertaking? The fact, I was told, is that there are vast brown coal deposits in the immediate neighborhood, but *not* directly underneath the compound area. The ground on which the Combine is being built is sandy and practically worthless, as in Stalinstadt.

While the old-established brown coal mining districts, especially at Halle-Merseburg and Borna-Meuselwitz (District of Leipzig), show signs of stagnation and may be headed for early exhaustion, the more recently developed Lausitz deposits in the District of Cottbus (which will feed the Black Pump Combine) are gaining in importance from one year to the next. In 1959, the comparative share of the three districts, in total production, was as follows: Halle, 38.8%; Lausitz, 33.9%; Borna and neighborhood, 27.3%. Under the present Seven-Year-Plan, the center of gravity, in brown coal production, is to shift steadily from the two other districts to the Lausitz whose share is expected to rise to 42% by 1965.

There are at least two good reasons for this geographical resolution in brown coal mining, even discounting the possibility that Halle and Borna may be running out of supplies some years hence (a question much in dispute among experts). For one thing, the brown coal of the Lausitz, having a low content of sulphur and ashes, is better suited to the refining processes for which the Black Pump Combine is being built. And, for another, the Lausitz holds about 63% of all brown coal deposits in the DDR that can be mined at or immediately below the surface, which is of course more economical than deep pit operations. The brown coal deposits of the Lausitz are believed to be the largest in Europe, with total reserves estimated at 30 billion tons.

Some 7.5 miles away from the industrial area — a distance considered necessary and sufficient to prevent the smoke and gas fumes from invading the workers' living quarters — another tailor-made "Socialist" model city after the pattern of Stalinstadt is in the making. Built on the outskirts of Hoyerswerda, it will house the Combine's labor force of 16,000 (after completion) and their families. The workers will commute to and from the plant by means of a fast electric railroad now under construction. A brief excursion to the new settlement showed that many rows of apartment houses have already gone up and others are in various stages of construction. However, they are not so distinctive as those in Stalinstadt, nor is the general layout of "Neu-Hoyerswerda" as impressive as that of Germany's "first Socialist city".

12

Schwedt:
Oil Town of Tomorrow

"300,000 tank waggons with a capacity of 25 tons each would be needed to transport the 7.5 million tons of mineral oil which the Soviet Union will deliver to the DDR in 1970 by pipeline," an East German Economic Ministry official had told me. So I wanted to find out for myself how much progress had been made to date on this ambitious scheme, one that involved the building of a huge transcontinental pipeline system stretching for thousands of miles through the Soviet Bloc.

For an on-the-spot report — insofar as East Germany's contribution to this undertaking was concerned — I made a trip to Schwedt, a small town on the Oder, some thirty miles upstream from the big port of Stettin (Szczecin) which is in Polish-administered territory. There, at Schwedt, one arm of the vast pipeline system now under construction is to end; other terminal points will be located in Poland, Hungary and Czechoslovakia.

At Schwedt, hitherto known only as the center of a tobacco-growing region and renowned for its fine princely palace (destroyed in the last war), a huge oil refinery, destined to be one of the largest in Europe, is in the process of construction. When completed in 1968 (if all goes according to plan), it will have a throughput capacity of eight million tons of crude annually, all of which is to come from Soviet Russia's "Second Baku", i.e. the far-flung oil-producing territory between the Volga and the Urals, by way of the transcontinental pipeline.

Long before that final target date, however, the Schwedt refinery, already dubbed somewhat prematurely "Erdölverarbeitungswerk Schwedt" (E.V.W.), is expected to be in partial operation. According to present plans, initial capacity is to be two million tons yearly in 1963 when the Soviet crude will begin to flow through the pipeline system in quantities. By 1965, a capacity of four million tons a year is to be reached.

Of the four principal development projects I visited, and which are described in the present volume, the Schwedt refinery is the youngest and therefore least advanced. Plans for the transcontinental pipeline system were drawn up in June 1958 at a meeting in Bucharest of the Soviet Bloc's "Council for Mutual Economic Aid", which in recent years has been coordinating all economic and industrial activities within the Soviet sphere. Details of where the East German terminal was to be built, how it was to be connected to the Polish end of the pipeline system, etc., were subsequently worked out in tripartite agreements between the governments of the Soviet Union, Poland and the DDR.

That Schwedt is the youngest of the four big new enterprises discussed here, is immediately apparent the moment one sets foot inside the works compound. Whereas at Stalinstadt, "Black Pump" and Rostock the visitor is received in spacious or even stately administration buildings, at Schwedt he meets the officials in charge in the cramped surroundings of a lowly barracks building.

The total area that has been staked off as building site for the refinery and future dependent installations covers no less than 16 square kilometers, I was informed. If this figure is accurate, it would mean that the planned dimensions of the Schwedt enterprise are almost double those of the "Black Pump" Combine's unless the latter, in reality, far exceeds the admitted Mueggelsee proportions (which I rather suspect). Of the 16 sq. km. set aside, one-fourth has so far been cleared of the pine and spruce native to this region.

As with the other projects I visited, I was also interested here in finding out what specific considerations had determined the selection of this particular building site. Four reasons were given me:

One, this region so far has been one of the least industrialized in the DDR; establishment of a large plant there will help redress the balance and in the process also (the Communist planners feel) end the cultural "backwardness" of this predominantly agricultural area, known as the "Uckermark".

Two, while almost everywhere in the country there is a crying shortage of labor, this hitherto underdeveloped farm country still offers certain reserves of manpower.

Three, the large amounts of water required for the operation of a big refinery are readily available from the nearby Oder river; the same also goes for a new paper plant being built on the fringe of the refinery area (it was due to go into production in the fall of 1961).

Four, with the gasoline, diesel and fuel oil to be produced at Schwedt it will be possible to supply more economically the northern part of the country which is comparatively far removed from Leuna and other producing centers heretofore existing.

A possible fifth determining factor may be seen in the peculiar strategic concept which I have already discussed in Chapter 10.

After the tract required for the refinery proper and related installations had been cleared and leveled in 1959 and through most of 1960, the ceremonial laying of the first stone for the refinery foundation took place on November 11, 1960. Since then, I observed, work has progressed rapidly at all levels.

The principal thoroughfare of the plant is ready in the rough; some ten miles of railroad track are in operation (out of a total rail network of about 40 miles planned); the foundations of the refinery and the power plants have been laid; some 25 oil tanks (one-fourth of the total planned), varying in size from 5,000 to 20,000 cubic meters, are finished or in the process of construction.

According to the chief engineer who accompanied me on my tour of the building site, there is no doubt that the first Soviet crude will flow through the pipeline by the end of 1962 and that the then partially completed Schwedt refinery will be ready to start processing it. Indeed, with all the resources of an authoritarian regime thrown behind it — for instance, the FDJ ("Free German Youth") organization was mobilized to take this building scheme under its wing as a so-called "youth project" — the Schwedt refinery is bound to be ready on time, regardless of cost. Yet again in this case, as so often, a host of unexpected difficulties the planners had failed to take into account began cropping up after the ground had been broken.

For instance, at Schwedt, the ground water level was found to be exceptionally high in places, making extensive drainage operations necessary. I had been wondering a bit whether the large pools of water I noticed in many places — some of them as large as village ponds — were a normal occurrence on a refinery building site. The accompanying engineer sadly shook his head. "It's our biggest worry," he admitted.

Special care must also be taken to prevent any oily waste from reaching the Oder on which the nearby city of Stettin depends for much of its drinking water. The Poles wouldn't like it and since the pipeline crosses their territory they could threaten to shut off the flow of crude if it spoilt their drinking water. The extra precautions made necessary by this situation will add about 30 million marks to the ordinary building costs, I learned.

In the initial phase of operations, lasting at least through 1965, the Schwedt refinery will turn out only gasoline (84 octane), diesel and heating oil. Further processing by catalytic methods and cracking will not take place until after the plant reaches full capacity in 1968; at that time facilities for making lubricants are to be added. Eventually, a special "oil port" is to be built on the banks of the Oder. There are no present plans to branch out into the field of petrochemicals since the facilities already existing at Leuna and elsewhere are deemed adequate to cover the country's requirements.

13

Collectivized Farming —
Will It Work?

Easily the most serious mistake the East German regime committed in shaping its economic policies has been the forced collectivization of agriculture in the spring of 1960.

With the diverse experiences of the Soviet Union, Poland, Czechoslovakia, Yugoslavia and Communist China there to guide him, Ulbricht should have known better than to attempt so radical a measure at a time when his regime, while fairly stable, was still far from being firmly rooted.

Peasants are stubborn people, everywhere in the world. They are also, as a rule, more pronounced individualists than townspeople are. And it is never easy to teach them new tricks.

It may be granted that the ultimate, long-range objective the East German Government has in mind is defensible. The fragmentation of agricultural holdings, which had become even more widespread after the agrarian reform of 1945-46 that broke up the big landowners' estates, did make for wasteful and inefficient farming, at least in some parts of the country.

Tractors, harvesting machines and other kinds of motorized

farming equipment are essential for raising the yield and the quality of crops, but their purchase is not within the reach of smallholders. Modern stables, with mechanized installations for feeding and watering cattle and horses, for milking cows and other farming chores are a big help, too, but how many individual peasants can afford such conveniences?

Collective farming which puts modern implements and facilities at the disposal of even the poorest peasant and which plans the distribution of crops in accordance with the expert advice of trained agronomists is certainly not a bad thing per se. It may even be an excellent one, though its superiority over individual farming methods has not been proven yet — even in the Soviet Union with its more than forty years of experience in this field.

When President Kennedy, in a recent address to the Canadian Parliament at Ottawa declared, "Fewer men on fewer acres than any nation on earth ... free men on free acres can produce here in North America all the food that a hungry world could use, while all the collective farms and forced labor of the Communist system produce one shortage after another ..." he certainly had a point.

As yet, not one collectivized farming system in the world has produced an economy of plenty. That is a fact. Why that is so, has just been demonstrated again forcefully in the case of East Germany.

Up to the end of 1959, collectivization in East Germany had been, by and large, on a voluntary basis. To be sure, the pressure to join an LPG ("Landwirtschaftliche Produktions-Genossenschaft" or Agricultural Production Cooperative) was always there, but as yet it had not taken the form of overt and irresistible coercion, as it did in the spring of 1960.

(Incidentally, there is a major difference between the Soviet kolkhozes and East Germanys LPG's. Whereas in the Soviet Union all land is the property of the state which grants a leasehold to the kolkhoz, in the DDR it is the cooperative (LPG) that owns the land. In a purely nominal sense, the members of the LPG even remain proprietors of their land and buildings and they have the right to withdraw from the cooperative. However, this is pure fiction, for in practice they cannot leave on pain of being expelled not only from their homes and village, but even from the territory of the DDR — to West Germany sometimes! — as happened in a number of cases in the summer of 1961. All things considered, the difference between a Soviet kolkhoz and an East German LPG would seem to be a purely technical one, devoid of real significance.)

In the course of the agrarian reform (revolution would be a more appropriate term, of course) of 1945-46 which led to the splitting-up of all large estates in excess of 100 hectares as well as of all land owned by former Nazis and Junkers, a total of three million hectares was expropriated and redistributed as follows: 967,000 hectares were turned over to the newly formed state farms or "people-owned estates"; 924,000 hectares were distributed among 119,000 so-called "landless peasants", many of them former laborers on the big estates of the gentry; 75,400 hectares were allotted to a total of 89,000 refugees; 72,000 hectares were used to increase the holdings of poor peasants; 43,000 hectares were leased to 50,000 smallholders; 110,000 hectares were set aside for the use of 170,000 craftsmen and 62,000 hectares of woodlands were distributed among 4,000 "old-established peasants".

About six years after the last of the feudal estates had been split up and parceled out into small peasant holdings, a process in reverse was launched. Beginning in July, 1952, the ruling Socialist Unity Party or SED started pushing the establishment of agricultural production cooperatives or LPGs on a large scale. There were to be three different kinds of these cooperatives, each ruled by a standard statute fixed by governmental degree.

In an LPG of Type I, the members were to pool only their holdings of arable land, retaining individual control of their livestock and machinery; Type II provided for collective use of machinery and beasts of draught as well; finally, in Type III, the "perfect type", all arable land, forest areas, livestock, pastures and machinery were to be thrown into the common fund of the cooperative. However, even in the case of this type of cooperative, which from the start was looked upon with greatest official favor, a minimum of private property was to be preserved: each peasant member was to be allowed to retain half a hectare of land for gardening purposes, one or two cows or horses, 2 to 5 pigs, and as many sheep, goats and poultry as he could provide for with fodder grown on his reserved half hectare of land.

Although all the resources of propaganda and persuasion were thrown behind the collectivization drive, the response of the East German farmers was at best half-hearted. Some 9,000 of them fled to Western Germany in the first two months of 1953 when pressure to join the agricultural cooperatives reached its first peak; the unsuccessful revolt that took place a few months later (June 17, 1953) undoubtedly was sparked at least in part by the farmers' resistance against collectivization.

In the years that followed, a go-slow policy was adopted by the regime, in this as in other controversial fields. While the number of LPGs throughout the country increased steadily, the progress of collectivization was not spectacular. From 12.3% in 1955, the share of the LPGs' in the gross national product rose to 16.7% in 1957; 25.3% in 1958; and 32.7% in 1959; in the same four-year period, the private sector in farming declined from 75.7% to 68.2%, then 60.3% and finally

52.4% while state farms went up only slightly from 12.0% in 1955 to 14.9% in 1959.

Thus, at the beginning of 1960, a little more than one-half of East Germany's agriculture was still in private hands. There were still some 600,000 independent peasant families at that time, many of them long-established settlers whose farms had been handed down from father to son for generations, others newcomers who had acquired their first taste of independent farming after 1945.

What prompted the East German Government, early in 1960, to turn the slow, but nevertheless continuous process of collectivization of the past eight years into a "crash program" of greatest urgency?

There were several reasons, though none of them is fully convincing. For one thing, the regime felt, with some measure of justification, that it had become largely stabilized since the upheaval of June, 1953, and that it could therefore move less cautiously and more in accordance with its ideological concepts. For another thing, there may have been a desire to prejudge the outcome of the East-West negotiations on Germany (with an eye on ultimate reunification) that were then in the offing by creating the accomplished fact of a completely "Socialized" agriculture in the DDR.

The technological progress achieved in the meantime — more tractors, more agricultural machinery of all kinds available — also spurred the Communist planners' hopes that more food could be produced more quickly on huge collective farms provided with the ultimate in mechanization and rationalization of tillage and husbandry.

Finally, there may have been some prodding from Moscow, for at the time the DDR had reached a combined Socialist sector of 48% in its agriculture, other Soviet satellites were able to report far more impressive percentages; Bulgaria, almost 100%; Albania, 85%; Czechoslovakia, 82%; Romania, 70%; Hun-

gary, 56%; only Poland was lagging far behind with a Socialist sector of only 15%, but then that country, by common con-
sent, was a special case. Anyway, for Walter Ulbricht, the
Communist oldtimer, it could be no source of satisfaction or
pride to find himself on the second-lowest rung of the collectivization ladder, between two such questionably Communist countries as Poland and Hungary.

At the seventh session of the central committee of the SED,
held December 10-13, 1959, it was decided to speed up the
process of collectivization by all means at the disposal of the
regime. In the four-months periods beginning on January 1st,
1960 and ending on the traditional holiday of Socialists, May
1st, more LPGs were to be formed and more land was to be
converted from private to cooperative use than in all the seven
and a half years that had gone before.

The ruthless drive launched at the start of the new year in
order to achieve this ambitious goal was successful, even
though the pretense of voluntary adhesion to the cooperatives
was not abandoned. While overt compulsion was not resorted
to, irresistible moral and political pressure was brought to
bear on reluctant farmers. Those who failed to heed admon-
ishments to join — some peasants were visited by as many as
five groups of agitators within a few days — were threatened
with prosecution for alleged black market activities or other
economic crimes; or they were simply told that in future no
artificial fertilizers, no seeds or other essential supplies and
no repair service for worn-out machinery would be available
for farmers outside the production cooperatives. In many instances, recalcitrant peasants were pilloried in the press or held
up to public scorn in meetings organized ad hoc.

In the face of such formidable pressure, resistance quickly
vanished. On March 5, 1960, the District of Rostock which had
been the first to initiate the all-out drive for collectivization
under the leadership of Karl Mewis, a trusted henchman of

Ulbricht's, reported the complete disappearance of the private farming sector. In the following weeks, all the other districts reported 100-percent collectivization in quick succession. Last to report this success, on April 14 — still well ahead of the deadline set by the party leadership — was the District of Karl-Marx-Stadt (Chemnitz).

The drive, then, had been a complete success — but at what cost! Tens of thousands of dispirited farmers fled to the West, while others sullenly accepted the inevitable, determined to make the best (for themselves) of a bad job. They had been told that as members of a cooperative, they would have an eight-hour workday and Sunday off — and now they stuck to it. Whereas, as free farmers, they used to be in the fields from dawn to dusk, sunshine or rain, when necessary, now they laid the implements aside when the eight hours were over and Sundays went fishing or on boating trips even though the crops were rotting in the fields.

As a result of this foreseeable reaction, which ranged from indifference to passive resistance, agricultural productivity fell off instead of increasing, valuable machinery was left untended and unrepaired, production schedules were not met and delivery quotas were not fulfilled. And before long, the gaps in the butcher shops, the recurring shortages of milk, butter and vegetables, the scarcity of that standard food, potatoes, brought home once more to the Marxist theorists what happens when the farmer goes on strike in that quiet but highly efficient way of his.

Khrushchev himself once has said, "You can't make pancakes (blinchiki) out of statistics". The East German housewives will gladly bear him out.

14

Anatomy of an "LPG": A Visit to the Agricultural Cooperative of Jahna

Having read quite a bit about the East German version of a kolkhoz, the agricultural production cooperative of LPG, I was naturally curious to get a close look at the inner workings of those newfangled establishments of the DDR countryside.

In response to my wish, my hosts arranged for a visit to the "Socialist Village of Jahna", one of the oldest and largest creations of this kind. It is located about two kilometers from the picturesque medieval town of Meissen in Saxony, with its world-famous cathedral and porcelain manufactory which were glimpsed in passing.

Properly speaking, Jahna is not one village, but a long-stretched agglomeration of villages, hamlets and outlying farmsteads now grouped together in one large cooperative unit comprising about 2,000 hectares. Most of its inhabitants (about 800 in Jahna proper) are resettlers from the lost German provinces in the east, especially Silesia, rather than people native to the soil.

This is doubtless one reason why the villagers of Jahna could be more easily prevailed upon to form a rural cooperative than has been the case in areas where the peasantry had been rooted for centuries. Few of the small farms, averaging five hectares, that had been carved out of the three large estates (Oberjahna, Niederjahna and Schlettau) broken up by the 1945 land reform, were viable units. So when the Communist party agitators came to Jahna in the summer of 1952 to plead for collectivization, they found the going comparatively easy. On August 8, 1952, the "LPG Walter Ulbricht, Jahna bei Meissen" was founded, taking its name (as did the Leuna Chemical Works and other industrial enterprises) from the Communist boss of East Germany.

How typical is Jahna of agricultural cooperatives in the DDR? I have often wondered about it and would not like to give a pat answer to that question. While I have no doubt that Jahna, which in its nine years of existence has had a fair chance to get properly organized, is a model cooperative and a sort of rural showplace, I don't think it would be fair to describe it as a unique specimen, much less as a "Potemkin village." Indeed, I have always found that the things I was shown in the DDR were perhaps models of their kind but by no means isolated specimens. Too many counterchecks persuaded me that what I saw was not only real but existed in several other places. On the other hand, it is plausible to assume that when my hosts took me to Jahna, they were going to show me the best there was in the field, not just something average or worse. No doubt there are other LPGs, especially those thrown together in haste since the beginning of 1960, that would not stand comparison with an old-established and advanced one like Jahna.

A leisurely tour of the cooperative, by car and on foot, showed that it is organized according to an exact (and, one might add, exacting) blueprint and functioning reasonably well in accordance with it. All the technical improvements of modern farming on a large scale are in evidence. There are big and well-kept stables with mechanized facilities for feeding, milking and other chores. A fair-sized MTS (machine-tractor station) on the Soviet model supplies the agricultural machinery needed and keeps it in repair. Incidentally, the fact that the LPG of Jahna exercises its own control of MTS operations, on a sort of lend-lease basis, shows that it is looked upon in official quarters as a well-run cooperative. Originally, all machine-tractor stations were set up by the state independently of the agricultural units they were destined to serve. In 1958, the government decided to let meritorious agricultural cooperatives take charge of a given MTS and lease its machinery. In the process, the "Traktoristen", as the personnel of an MTS are called, usually were invited to join the cooperative itself and share in all the benefits. This was also done at Jahna.

Presumably, the policy of making the "tractorists" join the cooperative they had been serving was also inspired by political considerations. For these men were for the most part well-indoctrinated city boys drawn from the ranks of the "Free German Youth" or some other organization affiliated with the ruling party who could be trusted to plug the right political line in the cooperative councils.

A great deal has been done at Jahna to facilitate the housework of the peasant women who for the most part also work in the fields and stables. There are many and excellently organized communal services, in particular a large, modern laundry which is one of the busiest places in the village (I was told it takes up to three weeks to get one's washing back); a well-stocked self-service store that makes daily shopping trips to Meissen unnecessary; and a very pleasant kindergarten. In addition, there is also a "Kinderhort" where the older children, after school hours, spend their leisure time, play games, do their homework and wait for their parents to get back from the fields.

It was at the kindergarten, where an attractive young nurse in a trim uniform, surrounded by a horde of neat and healthy-looking youngsters, showed us around, that I most strongly had the impression of a showplace organized as much for propaganda purposes as for its benefits to children. For the way this young lady reeled off the vital statistics of her establishment, even without being asked, clearly showed that she was used to receiving visitors and telling them all about the wonderful life at Jahna in general and at her kindergarten in particular. I don't doubt in the least that it is a fine place nor that she is doing a splendid job, but a little more spontaneity and a little less rehearsing would have helped mitigate the rather obvious political overtones of her performance.

When the Jahna cooperative was formed in 1952, some 70 peasants, or about one-half of those eligible for membership, joined up. They were for the most part the smallholders, with farms ranging from five to twenty hectares in size. In 1953, the year of the abortive "counter-revolution", no less than fifteen of them resigned from the LPG, I was candidly informed by an official of the cooperative. "However, in 1955 they all came back", he added.

When the all-out drive for collectivization began, early in 1960, the last remaining hold-outs, including a few "big peasants" (Grossbauern) who owned the legal maximum of 100 hectares, were quickly brought into line. Just in time for the deadline of May 1st, Jahna made it to the officially required 100 percent — not a very proud boast for one of the oldest LPGs in the country.

Only about one-half of the 600-odd members of the cooperative chose to retain for private cultivation the reserved half-hectare of land they all are entitled to, I was told. The others preferred to throw this tiny plot into the common pool, too (they are compensated for it, of course), while keeping a cow or two and a few pigs, as permitted.

To all practical purposes, the once independent farmers of Jahna today are salaried employees of a huge agricultural enterprise which they do, however, jointly own.* But perhaps "salaried" is not the right word, for the members of the cooperative are not paid fixed wages. They are compensated in accordance with an extremely complex payment system — one so involved that it requires the full-time services of one accountant and seven bookkeepers! (Needless to say, they also take care of the commercial operations of the cooperative.)

Members of agricultural cooperatives are paid according to the number of "work units" they earn in a year. The value of work units, as well as the time and effort required by them vary from one place to another. Each LPG has a so-called "Normenkommission" which fixes the work and payment norms in accordance with government directives and local requirements.

In the case of Jahna, one work unit is currently worth 10.50 marks, which is well above the average and legal minimum of 7.00 marks. Average annual earnings, I was told, run to 800 units for a working couple (600 thereof for the husband and 200 for the wife), or about 8,040 marks. In addition, such a couple is supposed to make another 4,000 through gardening, pig-and-poultry-raising and other uses of their reserved portion. They also receive from the common fund about 500 marks' worth of cereals, potatoes, vegetables and straw. All this adds up to a very handsome total — provided, of course, the figures are true and they truly refer to average earnings (I have some doubts on this score).

It will hardly come as a surprise to those already familiar

---

*Whenever the business of the cooperative yields a net profit in a year, members are paid dividends.

with Communist practice that it is the "white-collar workers" rather than the toilers in the field who earn the most money at Jahna. The president of the cooperative is allowed 1,080 units annually, his deputy, 960 units; the accountant gets 900 units and each of the seven bookkeepers makes 550. "Tractorists" and "brigade leaders" (of whom there are seven) earn 600 units each, while the highly rated "Viehpfleger" or cattle wardens who supervise the various livestock departments, and go by such names as "Schweinemeister" or pig master, may make as much as 700 units. By contrast, the annual earnings of field laborers, stable attendants and other menials are well below "average".

By and large, the men and women of Jahna appear to be fairly well off. Quite a few of them own private cars and nearly all of them possess at least a motorcycle. Their homes — some are still living in their old farmsteads while others are tenants in new houses built for them by the cooperative — are reasonably comfortable and well-furnished. Television sets are comparatively numerous.

For every 50 work units he or she earns a year, a member is entitled to one day of paid vacations, up to a maximum of 12 days. If the vacationer goes to a resort selected for him by the management — not many of them do — his board and travel expenses are paid for by the cooperative. Some of the members prefer private travel arrangements at vacation time, but the large majority simply stays put for a good rest at home.

15

Education and Culture

Education in the DDR is generally on a high level. The emphasis, as in the Soviet Union, is on technical proficiency, orthodox thinking and dialectics rather than on the humanities and an all-around formation of the spirit. One may argue, therefore, that much of what is being taught in DDR schools and colleges is hardly worth knowing at all, or is even detrimental to a young mind. But teaching methods, scholastic institutions and especially state expenditures for education easily stand comparison with the best that other countries have to offer.

Education at all levels is not only free (the last tuition fees, at the universities, were abolished as of January 1st, 1957), but heavily subsidized. Up to 90 percent of all college students live on scholarships provided by the state or state-controlled organizations. To be sure, not every young boy or girl who feels like it can count on getting a college education. Screening of applicants is severe and candidates are picked from the viewpoint of political trustworthiness as well as for their scholastic merits. Nevertheless, it is a fact that there are, in the DDR, nearly twice as many university students per capita

(5.1 for every 1,000 inhabitants) as there are in Western Germany (2.8 per 1,000).*

In considering these figures, one must bear in mind, however, that there are in the DDR two kinds of students, the "Direktstudenten" who regularly attend classes at a university or college, and the "Fernstudenten" who learn by correspondence school methods while working in a factory, in an office or on a cooperative farm. Discounting the latter category, the picture is more evenly balanced for the two parts of Germany, but even so the DDR is in the lead with a percentage of 38.2 per 10,000, as compared to West Germany's 30.3 for all kinds of academic institutions (universities, institutes of technology, specialized colleges etc.).†

On the lower levels, the traditional German system of popular education has been completely revamped in the DDR and it is now totally different from the one still existing in the Federal Republic. Both the "Volksschule" or elementary school and the "Gymnasium" or high school have been done away with. In their stead, an altogether novel type of school, combining elementary and secondary education over a ten-year period and known as "polytechnische Oberschule" (polytechnic high school), has been established of late.

True, the polytechnic high school system is not yet everywhere in existence. As a model to be universally adopted in time, it has been introduced in the most "advanced" places such as Stalinstadt, "Germany's first Socialist City". A law passed by the People's Chamber on December 2, 1959, provides that beginning in 1964 all children must attend this type of school from their sixth to their sixteenth years. A characteristic hallmark of the polytechnic high school is the strong ac-

---

*Cf. *"Studium bei Freunden"* published by the DDR State Secretariat for Higher Education.

†*Statistisches Taschenbuch der DDR* for 1960.

cent on mathematics and natural sciences, as well as selected subjects of technology. There are also practical courses in agricultural and industrial production. Classical languages are not taught and among modern foreign language courses the teaching of Russian predominates.

In the interim, an experimental system developed after 1946, with an eight-year elementary and a four-year high school, still functions widely in the DDR. Needless to say, there are no private or religious schools.

One of the major objectives of the East German school reformers has been, from the start, to break what they call "the monopoly on education", meaning that in capitalist countries only the children of the privileged classes have access to higher education. Although this is a typical Marxist cliché long ago discarded by reality — there certainly has not been any "monopoly on education" in the United States for a long time — it is still being solemnized in the DDR as elsewhere in the Soviet Bloc.

Admission to universities and other institutions of higher learning is therefore largely dependent not only on the political convictions of the applicant but also on his social origins. The son of a worker or peasant will always find it easier to get into college, in the DDR, than would a boy of unmistakably bourgeois descent. According to the latest issue of the DDR "Statistical Pocket Book", the social distribution of "direct students" at institutions of higher learning, in 1959, was as follows: 51.4% were children of working-class parents; 5.5% came of peasant stock; 19% were sons and daughters of white collar workers; 14.9% were the offspring of intellectuals and the remaining 9.2% were classed as "others".

In the course of my trip, I visited several school buildings, in various parts of the country, and I must say that I found them to be, almost without exception, in perfect condition, with bright modern classrooms, well-lighted and aired, and equipped with everything needed for teaching, technical training, recreation and sports. In many schools, the children are also served meals.

In view of what I have seen in the DDR, I find no reason to doubt the East German Government's claim that it spends, on a per capita basis, four or five times as much on higher education, vocational training and scientific research as the Federal Republic.

One of the most interesting institutions of higher learning I visited in the DDR was the "Institut für Ausländerstudium" or International College of Leipzig, one of the many, widely-scattered departments of the 552-year-old university which, under Communist management, has been renamed "Karl-Marx-Universität."

This College, a fine complex of modern buildings located on what used to be Dölnitzerstrasse but now is "Lumumba Street" — a change of name full of significance — serves to acquaint foreign students with the language and culture of Germany (and, incidentally, with the rudiments of Marxist-Leninist ideology) in preparation for further study at East German universities or specialized colleges.

At present, the vast majority of the foreign students who attend classes there are natives of the new nations of Africa and Asia. In talks with school officials, I encountered a certain reluctance to discuss in detail the nationality, social origin or identity of the students.

"We wouldn't want any of our boys to get into trouble", one of the officials remarked, hinting that quite a few students from countries that did not maintain cordial relations with the Soviet bloc had enrolled at the Institute without the knowledge or approval of their respective governments.

I gathered, however, that citizens of "non-committed" nations such as India, Indonesia, Iraq, Egypt, Syria, Ghana, Guinea and so forth, currently form a majority of the student body, far outnumbering both the nationals of pro-Western and Soviet bloc countries.

With very few exceptions, these foreign students are guests of the East German Government which not only pays for their board and tuition but also provides them with substantial scholarships, averaging 280 marks monthly, for their private expenses. As yet, the ratio of men to women, at the Institute, is very lopsided, the fair sex being outnumbered at least 10 to 1; but the trend is towards a more even balance of the sexes in the future.

In cultural matters, too, the East German regime constantly gives proof of an open-handedness unmatched in the West; by no means all of it can be shrugged off as "propaganda" though much of it, of course, pursues that aim. Again, I find it hard to quarrel with the claim (put forward in the Statistical Pocketbook for 1960) that state expenditures for cultural purposes, in particular the theater and music, are two or three times as high, per head in the population, as they are in West Germany. (The discrepancy, incidentally, is claimed to be even higher in the health services and children's care as well as public welfare generally.)

As a sample of the lavish spending for cultural purposes let me cite the case of the new opera house in Leipzig which was inaugurated on October 8, 1960. A leisurely tour of the building, followed by attendance at a performance − not an opera but the play "Egmont" by Goethe − showed the new Leipzig Opera to be not only the largest, but also one of the most luxuriously furnished and technically best-equipped theaters of its kind in Europe. Aside from the building costs of about five million marks, the government contributes an annual operating subsidy that works out at something like five marks per person and night, even though the Opera, with a capacity of 1,678 seats, is booked full most of the time at a yearly average of 92 percent.

16

Broadcasting and
The Press

"I am Konrad's troubadour, tra la la, I'm the Chancellor's darling boy . . ."

The sonorous voice booms so loud, I have to tune down my portable radio, for the hour is late. My car is parked in a quiet square in Hamburg. I am listening to a musical show heavily spiced with political propaganda, broadcast by — "the enemy", the "Deutschlandsender" of East Berlin.

A policeman walks by. He cocks a suspicious eye in my direction, wrinkles his brow. Let him. This is a free country. I can tune in on anything I want to hear. Even a show that makes fun of the government of this country.

A short while ago, I was sitting in another car, in East Germany, listening to the radio. The automobile, a flashy black limousine "Tatra 603" imported from Czechoslovakia, and its chauffeur, a burly, former Wehrmacht officer, had been put at my disposal by my East German hosts for my 1,000-mile round trip through the DDR.

The driver was turning the dial on the car radio, trying to get some nice music. Now he had settled on a station that was broadcasting something everybody likes to hear — Viennese

waltzes. Suddenly the announcer broke in: "This is Rias, Berlin." You should have seen the start the driver gave me as he
quickly turned the dial to another station. I don't blame him.
It wouldn't have been healthy for him to be caught listening
to an "enemy broadcast".

"I am Konrad's troubadour, tra la la, I'm the Chancellor's
darling boy . . ."

The ditty, sung by a throaty tenor, made fun of Willy
Brandt, Social-Democratic leader and Mayor of West Berlin.
The catchy tune, a clever text to match, and a variety of noises
interspersed by the singer all added up to the suggestion of an
obscene relationship existing between the old Chancellor and
his comparatively youthful opponent in the then impending
West German general election.

This is typical of the utterly unrestrained kind of propaganda war waged by the East German radio (and press)
against the leaders of the Federal Republic. No insinuation is
too cheap, no insult too gross, no sarcasm too heavy when it
comes to attacking Adenauer, Strauss, Brandt or any other of
the Communists' pet peeves. The coarseness of the language
used by East German commentators when dealing with West
German political figures must be heard to be believed. A gut-
tersnipe's vocabulary would sound refined by comparison. As
the Berlin crisis has mounted, so has the crescendo of invec-
tive.

While broadcasting, like every other means of communica-
tion in the DDR, is completely under the thumb of Communist opinionmakers, technically it is on a high level. The East
German transmitters are, for the most part, more powerful
than their opposite numbers in the West. About three-fourths
of the Federal Republic are blanketed by the East German
broadcasting network and in many parts of West Germany
the DDR's television programs appear on the screens more
neatly than any of those locally produced. In the course of

my travels through the Federal Republic, I encountered many places where the only broadcast clearly heard on my portable radio came from the DDR.

Radio and television are highly centralized in East Germany. All program directives emanate from, and most programming is done at, the huge, recently completed Broadcasting Center of Oberschöneweide, a suburb of East Berlin, where the "Staatliches Rundfunkkomitee" or State Broadcasting Committee, has its seat. Head of the Committee is Professor Hermann Ley, but the real key figure in the setup is his first deputy, Prof. Gerhart Eisler, a veteran Communist agitator who spent many years in the United States and eventually jumped bail while awaiting trial on charges aired before the House Committee on Un-American Activities.

While in East Berlin, I obtained permission to visit the heavily guarded Broadcasting Center, where few Western reporters ever are admitted. It is an imposing establishment where a high degree of technical proficiency meets the eye everywhere. The sprawling building is located on a vast site between Nalepa Street and the Spree River, at Oberschöneweide. It is reputed to be one of the most modern and best-equipped broadcasting houses in Europe. In the main concert hall, one notes a giant organ, said to be the largest ever built in this hemisphere.

What intrigued me most, however, was a walk through that fascinating portion of the establishment where every conceivable kind of noise, such as footsteps on a gravel path, a door being opened stealthily, or the hullabaloo of a drinking party are produced artificially amidst soundproof surroundings. The pride of this department is a "genuine" old German wine cellar, complete with an enormous wine barrel, shiny tankards and roughhewn wooden chairs. It is all for makebelieve, though. The only time wine flowed in that cellar — but how it flowed then! — was when the Broadcasting Center was inaugurated a few years ago. That must have been quite a party, judging by a series of woodcuts on display in which an artist has commemorated the festive event. The last in the row looks like a battlefield scene, except that the lifeless bodies strewn all over the floor are merely "Bierleichen" (beer corpses) as the Germans say of a drunk who has passed out cold.

Under one roof at the Oberschöneweide Center are the executive and administrative divisions of the three principal branches of the East German broadcasting system. They are: "Radio DDR," a country-wide network broadcasting mainly for domestic consumption; the "Deutschlandsender," whose powerful transmitters beam propaganda to the Federal Republic; and the East Berlin Radio. Television programs are also produced there, but the transmitting station is located elsewhere.

In talks with officials of the Center, I learned that there are now 44 transmitters in operation in the DDR, one long wave, three short waves, 19 medium waves and 21 ultra short waves. There are 5.5 million licensed radio sets and more than a million TV sets in the country.

Broadcasts in foreign languages are made daily by Radio Berlin International ("The Voice of the German Democratic Republic"). They are intended mainly for the non-aligned nations of Africa and Asia and are beamed to them in English, French and Arabic. The Scandinavian languages are also cultivated assiduously, for Denmark and Sweden, in particular, are favorite targets of East German propaganda.

I asked one leading official whether it was true that East Germany operates a large number of jamming transmitters — their number has been estimated as high as 600 by Western experts — for the purpose of drowning out the voice of RIAS (Radio in the American Sector), the powerful, U.S.-supported transmitter in West Berlin which operates on several frequencies on all wave bands.

"We are not jamming them", he replied. "The fact of the matter is that they, in complete disregard of international agreements on broadcasting, transmit on wavelengths that have been assigned to us. So naturally we use those wavelengths too, and the result is a bit of disturbance in the air."

Whatever the truth of these charges may be, RIAS continues to get through, in spite of all attempts at interference. In the border areas and in East Berlin, West German telecasts are also received fairly well. In Thuringia, in particular, there used to be many East German viewers for the TV broadcasts from the powerful Ochsenkopf (ox-head) transmitter recently installed on a peak in the Fichtelgebirge Mountains of West Germany by the Bavarian Radio.

After the closing of the Berlin intra-city border, on August 13, 1961, the East German authorities launched a concerted drive against the owners of receiving sets equipped with antennae that enabled them to hear or see Western broadcasts. Dubbed "ox-heads" or "spiritual border crossers", such people now are being harassed by every means at the disposal of the regime. In many cases, their antennae have been forcibly removed or turned around in the direction of an East German transmitter by "Free German Youth" squads or by the police.

An example of the DDR's international radio programming (from *Foreign Affairs Bulletin* of July 24, 1962, official East German publication):

Listen To Radio Berlin International
The Voice of the German Democratic Republic

All transmissions can be heard daily including Sunday

Listeners in South-East Asia can tune in

from 16.30 to 19.30 Indian Standard Time	on the 19.73 metre band
from 17.30 to 20.30 Burmese Time	15,210 kilocycles
from 19.30 to 22.30 Indonesian Time	

The programmes commence and end with 15 minutes each in the German language; the rest of the transmissions are in the English language.

Half-hour transmissions in the English language can be heard daily on the same frequencies at the following times:

from 21.30 to 22.00 hours Indian Standard Time

from 22.30 to 23.00 hours Burmese Time

from 24.30 to 01.00 hours Indonesian Time

Listeners in Africa can tune in to English language transmissions daily

from 4.15 to 5 p.m. Greenwich Mean Time, that is) on the 24.98 metre band;

from 5.15 to 6 p.m. British Summer Time ⟨   12,008 kilocycles

17

Newspapers
Without News

Back in Berlin for a few hours, en route from Saxony to the Baltic coast, I casually told my East German companions one Sunday afternoon, "I guess I'll skip across the line (into the Western sectors) for a couple of hours. I am positively starved."

"What!?!" Their startled outcry was genuine enough.

"Do you really mean to say you didn't get enough to eat over here?" one of them asked incredulously. Another eyed me suspiciously: "It seems to me you've put on weight since you came to this country." (He was quite right, I had gained at least one pound in the first week I spent in the DDR.)

"That's not what I mean," I replied. "What I am starved for is news. After reading nothing but your papers for a whole week, I haven't the faintest notion of what goes on in the world these days. I've got to spend an afternoon catching up on the week's news".

They didn't relish that explanation either, of course, but let it go at that. It was not the first time I had told them plainly what I thought of their press, even though I felt a bit sorry to hurt the professional feelings of my hosts. But I feel strongly about honest reporting and the freedom of the press — both of which are nonexistent in the DDR.

131

Even to one long accustomed to the shortcoming of West German newspapers, reading the East German press comes as a shock.

It is not only tedious and dreary beyond belief, but also so packed with propaganda that the thin factual content of a "news story" simply gets lost in the welter of controversy. The cardinal sin of the newspaper business, slanting the news, is not only freely engaged in but it actually has been made a sacred obligation of East German journalists by the powers-that-be.

Even while I was in the DDR, Friedrich Ebert, Mayor of East Berlin and one of the top men of the regime, textually declared at a press festival: "The Socialist journalist must be first and foremost a political functionary. It is his duty to look upon his journalistic activity as an integral part of organized and planned party work". Could there be a more horrible concept of journalism than that?

In a purely nominal sense, there is a certain variety of newspapers, all of which, however, are tied up with one or the other of the various licensed political parties or "mass organizations". Actually, just as the multi-party system in the DDR is nothing but a sham and a fraud, since all parties and organizations are satellites of the all-powerful Socialist Unity Party or SED, so this apparent diversity of public opinion is nothing but a façade.

Whether you read one of the 16 official organs of the SED, or any of the 22 (for the most part much smaller) newspapers put out by the other parties and by the mass organizations, you always get the same lean, highly colored and heavily spiced fare.

All newspapers get their "news" from a single source — the Communist-controlled East German news agency ADN. All methodically distort whatever happens in the world in order to make it fit in the Communist scheme of things. All proclaim their allegiance to the spurious brand of democracy practiced in Soviet bloc countries. All are relentlessly subjected to the iron fist of censorship. All write in that peculiar, dogmatic and doctrinaire jargon which the West Germans have aptly dubbed "Parteichinesisch" (Party Chinese) because it sounds so involved and unintelligible to a normal person. All are virtually alike. Read one and you know what all 38 of the DDR's daily papers will print that day.

Even so it may happen, usually by accident rather than by design, that a paper scores what we would call a scoop. I learned of one such case, and a most recent one at that, quite by chance while I was staying in Leipzig. There, an interview with one of the most prominent editors of the DDR, Prof. Hans Teubner, had been arranged for me.

As I sat talking to Teubner, a spare, scholarly-looking man of middle age, I noticed on his desk the picture of a smiling young fellow in bathing trunks basking at the riverside with his attractive wife and baby daughter. There was no mistaking the boyish features and happy grin of Major Yuri Gagarin, Spaceman No. 1.

"I never saw this picture before", I told Prof. Teubner. "Where did you get it?"

Instantly his earnest face lit up with professional pride. He reached into his desk and pulled out a whole sheaf of original photos showing Gagarin and his kin in all kinds of free-and-easy poses at home, on a farm, on the street and so forth. Teubner then told me how, by a sheer stroke of editor's luck, he had come into possession of a priceless collection of exclusive photos featuring the Man-of-the-Hour. Within a few hours after the first announcement of Gagarin's successful venture into space had come over the radio, Teubner's paper, the *Leipziger Volkszeitung*, hit the streets with a one-page "extra" blaring the sensational news under giant bannerlines.

No sooner had this special edition appeared, than Teubner's

phone rang. At the other end of the wire was a woman who identified herself as Nadeshda Kirilowna Tschekotschikin and said she was a cousin of Yuri Gagarin's now living in Leipzig. She happened to have with her an album of family pictures made a year ago while she and the Gagarins were spending some time together at Glasna, a village not far from Moscow, she said, and added that she would be only too glad to turn these pictures over to the *Leipziger Volkszeitung* for publication, if the editors cared to have them.

Hearing this, Prof. Teubner, like a veritable provincial, immediately rushed over in person to Madame Tschekotschikin's Leipzig home to interview this relative of the world's No. 1 celebrity of the hour and to collect her priceless hoard of pictures. These were published in the next regular edition of the paper and made quite a hit.

"I was swamped with requests for republication rights not only from our own papers but also from the foreign press", Prof. Teubner happily assured me and I can well believe it. However, one scoop does not make a normally pale paper colorful nor does it bring much zest to a form of journalism that is conceived merely as a function of party work.

Besides being editor of one of the most influential papers in the DDR, Prof. Teubner is also a teacher at the country's only School of Journalism, the "Fakultät für Journalistik" of the Karl-Marx-University. It is now headed by Professor Dr. Hermann Budzislawski, a former liberal journalist whom I happened to know slightly from the days of the old "Weltbühne", to which we both contributed in the days of the Weimar Republic and while it was being published in exile during the Hitler regime. So I naturally dropped over for a chat and to see what a Communist-run school of journalism looks like. Needless to say, I didn't find it any more exciting than the newspapers it trains the new crop of editors to put out.

18

Bautzen:
Capital of Symbolism

In conclusion, a few impressions from one of the most peculiar of East German cities, Bautzen. As one wanders about the crooked, cobbled streets of this quaint old town in the southeastern corner of Saxony, he may well wonder at times where he is. Street signs, name plates, public notices are couched in a strange idiom the visitor, even one well-versed in foreign languages, may never have heard of before.

At the top of the tower of the new post office building in the central square of Bautzen, there appears, underneath the German inscription "Deutsche Post", the strange lettering "Némski Póst". Around the corner, the door plate on a stately building, newly constructed in the traditional style of the region, proclaims this to be the "House of the Sorbs" and the seat of the "Domowina". Next door, a pleasant coffee-house identified as "Sorb Café", announces its opening and closing hours, on a sign displayed in the center window, in the same mysterious togue.

All this sounds Slav, rather than German — and it is. Bautzen is the capital of a district where one of the most peculiar racial minorities in Europe lives — the Wends or Sorbs. This racial splinter, now numbering about 40,000 persons, although by official count there were twice as many at the end of World War II, represents the rather pitiful remnant of a once mighty tribe that used to live in these parts long before they were subdued by German conquerors in the 12th and 13th centuries.

The Wends or Sorbs are related to the Poles or Czechs rather than to the Serbs of Yugoslavia, as their name would seem to indicate. For a while, in the early stage of occupation after the last war, some Sorb leaders agitated in Moscow, in the name of Slav kinship, for union with Czechoslovakia. They never got to first base though, because Czechoslovakia at the time was still a "bourgeois" country and Stalin suspected (rightly, one might add) that the Sorbs' eagerness for a sort of "Anschluss" in reverse was inspired less by any "racial" motive than by a wish to get out from under the Communist rule in East Germany. By the time Czechoslovakia itself had fallen to Communist rule, the Sorb irredentist movement was dead and nothing came of the scheme.

However, the East German Government, bowing as usual to a Moscow directive, decided to use the existence of this tiny racial group for setting an example of how well treated national minorities are under Communism. And so the Sorbs — they live for the most part in the "Lausitz" region between Cottbus and the Czechoslovak border, though some of them are scattered as far north as the Spreewald (Spree River Forest) — were granted full cultural autonomy within the framework of the Communist society they have been forced to stay in.

Although the number of people who profess to be Sorbs has declined sharply since the war — this is the main reason why their official number has dropped in 15 years to one-half its previous level — the teaching of the Sorb language in East German schools has actually increased. In the District of Cottbus for instance, there are now 121 Sorb teachers against 54 in 1952. Altogether, there are at present 110 Sorb schools with a total enrollment of 5,000 pupils and 600 teachers. Several newspapers and magazines are published in the Sorb language and even books printed in this little-known idiom are put out by the state-run publishing houses. The Sorbs also have their own miniature Parliament, the "Domowina", but of course it has no more rights and privileges than any other of the rubber-stamp assemblies in the Soviet bloc.

The humorous part of it all is that this official fuss about racial minority rights and cultural autonomy goes far beyond what the Sorbs themselves asked for. With very few exceptions, they have long since become so fully Germanized that they speak, read, and write German much better than their supposedly native tongue. True, they stick to their old traditions and customs, their folklore, and their picturesque dresses (worn mostly on festive occasions), but they usually converse in German among themselves as with the German population element. Therefore, the use of bilingual street signs and official inscriptions can at best be described as an act of symbolism without practical importance.

Most people in the area regard the whole thing as a huge joke. When this writer, on a visit to the "Sorb Café", attempted to elicit some bits of information about the Sorb language from waiters and customers, it turned out that nobody present — including the Slavic-looking girl behind the pastry counter, who was also put to the test — spoke the mystery language fluently, or anywhere near it. All of them, by contrast, "saxonized" their German, as the Germans say in reference to the peculiar soft dialect spoken by the Saxons.

Apart from being the make-believe capital of a Red wonderland of symbolism, the importance of Bautzen is rather limited. There is little industry, while old handicrafts, such as glass blowing, still are practiced. It is an attractive tourist center, though, with a fine medieval castle, historic monuments, and lovely shady walks along still waterways.

In West Germany, Bautzen has still another reputation and a most unenviable one at that. It is supposed to hold one of the grimmest East German penitentiaries for political prisoners. When I asked an official where it was located, he looked at me blankly.

A penitentiary? Never heard of such a thing. Maybe it was the local reform school I had in mind . . .

Part 3

**East Germany's
Maritime Challenge**

19

Where the Flag
Follows Trade

On February 14, 1960, the port authorities of Hamburg witnessed an unusual spectacle. As the 6,500-ton freighter *Dresden* (10,000 tons deadweight) entered the harbor, she was flying two German flags of varying design. At the ship's foremast, the flag of the Federal Republic of Germany, in plain black, red, and gold, was hoisted, while from her stern the same colors, with a hammer and compass superimposed on them, were fluttering in the breeze.

This is the new flag of the DDR which was adopted by the Communist regime on September 21, 1959. Denounced by the West Germans as a "Spalterflagge" (separatist flag), it has been practically, though not officially, banned on the territory of the Federal Republic. However, it cannot be kept out of West German waters ruled by international status, such as the Free Port of Hamburg, the Kiel Canal, or the network of inland waterways connecting the two parts of Germany with each other and with Czechoslovakia.

It is customary for a ship entering a foreign harbor to pay her respects to the host country by raising the latter's national flag from the foremast, while flying her own national colors from the stern. What was so unusual in the case of the *Dresden* was that this vessel, by following international usage, clearly demonstrated — for the first time — that the East German authorities no longer consider Western Germany a separate portion of one and the same nation, but rather as a foreign country.

The broad significance of this small event was not lost on the West German press and public. "Zonenschiff grüsst Bundesrepublik als Ausland" (Ship from the Eastern Zone Salutes Federal Republic As Foreign State), the Hamburg papers noted the following day in regretful astonishment. Though comments were few, the impression prevailed that a fiction maintained for ten years had been abandoned at last — by the other German side, anyway. The arrival of the *Dresden* in Hamburg Harbor put the finishing touches to a painful, but undeniable, historical process: the formation of two German states completely independent of each other and linked more by mutual antagonism than by the past bonds of a common race, language, culture and history.

Regardless of how the Bonn Government and the West in general may feel about it, barring the outbreak of another major war, it appears certain that the world will see a good deal of the new East German flag in the years ahead. Already it is being flown at international trade fairs and sports events, causing no end of unpleasant incidents but slowly making headway throughout the world.

But the surest way for the East German regime to win attention, and eventually recognition, for its flag is to put it on the high seas in a big way. For nothing short of a shooting war or blockade can prevent any country from showing on the oceans whatever colors or symbols it chooses to display.

All the East German Communists need for that purpose is ships — and ships is what they are after. In order to build seagoing ships, you have to have big shipyards — and big shipyards have been springing up in the DDR. In order to keep ocean-going vessels coming and going, you need modern ports with facilities for overseas shipping — and harbor construction work is being pushed vigorously all along East Germany's Baltic coast. All of these items — shipyard construction, port development, shipbuilding and the purchase of vessels for sale — are getting top priority in the current economic planning of the Grotewohl-Ulbricht Government.

There are several reasons why the East Germans, who, like their Russian masters, traditionally are "landlubbers" with limited seafaring and fishing interests, should have decided to take to the high seas in a big way. For one thing, the foreign trade of the DDR has been expanding mightily in recent years. According to the latest available figures, the country's total volume of foreign trade in 1959 amounted to 17.3 billion (East) marks, an overall increase of 15% over the preceding year, as compared to a gain of only 4.2% between 1957 and 1958.

Yet it was on the basis of the estimated figures for 1957 that the East German Government, in the late summer of 1957, decided to go ahead with an ambitious program of maritime expansion, primarily for the purpose of saving foreign exchange. At that time, it was estimated that about one-fifth of the country's foreign commerce was seaborne and that all but 5% of the total was being shipped in foreign bottoms. Approximately 22% of the foreign exchange earned in a year was being spent on chartering and transit fees.

Indeed, in the words of an official East German journal, "our country has been spending about 800 million rubles annually — mostly in dollars and pounds — on the chartering of foreign ships and on transit charges in foreign ports." By way of illustration, this paper reported that "it costs us 70,000 dollars to import 2,000 tons of Egyptian cotton via Hamburg!"

It is therefore the avowed policy of the East German Government to expand both the country's seagoing merchant fleet and its port facilities to the point of self-sufficiency. As Karl

Mewis, a member of the Central Committee of the ruling
SED and the Government's chief policy-making official in the
Baltic area, has put it: "Making our merchant marine independent of Hamburg and Stettin will help us save millions in
foreign exchange and will represent a big stride forwards toward the final victory of socialism."

On another occasion, Herr Mewis, in a talk to shipyard
workers at Stralsund, declared: "Building seagoing ships is
also a matter of first-rate political importance, for the acquisi-
tion of a fleet will ensure us world prestige and will sooner
or later lead to the recognition of our country by the capitalist
world."

Here, the East German leader put the finger on *one* of the
political considerations that are behind the maritime expansion drive of the DDR, alongside of the economic factors involved. Ships carry prestige, and they carry it to the far corners of the earth. Undoubtedly, the DDR's primary concern,
to be accepted as a legitimate state and an equal among equals
in the comity of nations, will be advanced materially by the
existence of a substantial fleet under its flag as well as by the
development of at least one major port accessible to big ships
of all nations.

Another, less outspoken and negative consideration is this:
By building up powerful competition in the vicinity of Hamburg, the East German Communists are striving to strike a
severe blow at that flourishing West German metropolis. If
they are successful in this endeavor, and Western Germany's
largest and most prosperous city some day — surely in the
rather distant future — is brought to the edge of ruin by concerted Soviet bloc boycott and competition, this will indeed
be a big gain for the Communist cause.

20

Rostock: Biggest Shipping
Center of the DDR

There was good reason, therefore, to select as last major stop on my round trip through the DDR the Baltic seaport of Rostock where I proposed to visit two important places: (1) the Warnowwerft, biggest shipyard in the country; and (2) the new "Overseas Port" under construction on the southern shore of the "Breitling" Lagoon between the city of Rostock proper and its outlet on the Baltic, Warnemünde. (This old fishing village and seaside resort, which used to be an autonomous community, now forms an integral part of the township of Rostock). A secondary purpose was to catch a glimpse of beach life at Warnemünde, one of DDR's most popular vacation areas.

In their search for a Baltic harbor that could be developed into a major overseas shipping center, the East German planners at first had fixed their attention on Wismar, westernmost of those already in existence on the territory of the DDR. As early as 1948, the Soviet Military Administration ordered the harbor basin of Wismar to be enlarged and deepened (from

6.5 to 9.5 meters). At the same time, a new channel, 15 kilo-meters long and 40 meters wide, was built from Timmendorf, near Wismar. A new quay of 600 meters length was installed in the basin. These improvements allowed the simultaneous handling of three ships of 10,000 dwt., where previously only small vessels of up to 2,000 tons were able to dock at Wismar Harbor.

More recently, the harbor of Wismar has been endowed with modern facilities for potash shipments, permitting an annual volume of 600,000 tons to be handled there. Since 1958, a special oil port has been under construction. As a result of these measures, the total volume of cargo handled by the port of Wismar rose steadily from 969,900 tons in 1955 to 1,246,100 in 1956; 1,604,700 in 1957 and 1,696,000 in 1958.

As yet, Wismar is the biggest port of the DDR, well ahead of its nearest rival, Rostock. Before long, however, Wismar will have to take a back seat and let Rostock instead take the honor of becoming the DDR's first overseas port and its "gate-way to the World."

There were at least two good reasons why Wismar would not stand the test of the role it had been intended for. In the first place, the harbor basin remains too small for large-scale overseas shipping and it cannot be expanded further. And, secondly, the network of roads, railroads and waterways available for further transportation of the cargo transshipped through this port is quite inadequate for a substantially increased volume of goods.

To be sure, the latter difficulty also exists in the case of Rostock, which also lacks good connections with its hinterland. Here, however, there was the possibility of building from scratch a brand new port tailored to the needs of overseas shipping. With Stralsund also out of the running, much for the same combination of factors that ruled out Wismar, Rostock was left as the best of three poor choices.

After all the pros and cons had been duly weighed and de-
bated, the policy-making Central Committee of the SED, at
its 33rd meeting, in November 1957, decided to shelve current development plans for Wismar and instead concentrate
on making Rostock into a big overseas port.

Rostock is not, properly speaking, either a coastal town or
a seaport. It is situated at the southern end of an irregularly
shaped lagoon called "Breitling" which is formed by the river
Warnow before it flows into the Baltic at Warnemünde. The
distance between the two towns is about nine miles.

It would have been impracticable to try to enlarge the old
harbor of Rostock, which is hemmed in by the old town. Even
if the latter were practically razed, there would not be enough
room, at this spot, for a harbor basin of sufficient size plus the
necessary area for docks, warehouses, silos, tank farms etc.
Nor did it seem feasible to expand the small port of Warnemünde, or to create an overseas harbor adjoining it on the Baltic coast. For in the absence of sheltering mountains and bays,
such an "outer harbor" would have been exposed to the unbroken fury of storms and high tides. A number of other considerations also made such a project inadvisable.

As a result, the East German Government decided instead
to build the overseas port on the southern shore of the main
portion of the "Breitling", which at this point resembles a
roughly quadrangular lake. Here there is plenty of space, both
ashore and in the water. There is a small village, called Petersdorf, but otherwise this area is generally uninhabited — a
blend of heath and red-covered moorland, the home of countless wild ducks. The site is approximately equi-distant from
the former city limits of Rostock and Warnemünde.

In order to make the prospective overseas harbor accessible
to large vessels, it was necessary to dig an entirely new channel through the "Hohe Düne" (High Dune) that separates the
Breitling from the Baltic. For, the natural passage formed by

the lower course of the river Warnow, which had been previously used by ships entering or leaving the harbor of Rostock, cannot be navigated by large vessels. Moreover, it allows only for one-way traffic at one time and the harbor entrance is narrowed by heavy silting.

The artificial channel, running parallel to the river passage, was to be five kilometers long and 10.5 to 11 meters deep, with a width of 60 meters at the sole (four more than the Suez-Canal at the time), permitting the unhampered passage of 10,000-ton ships in two-way traffic. In order to protect this waterway against high winds and waves, a new East Mole had to be built from scratch. (The old breakwater previously known as the East Mole now forms the West Mole of the new channel; it divides the two passages, the natural and the artificial one, both of which will be used by shipping.)

Even before the final decision had been made against Wismar and in favor of Rostock, work began on the latter project on October 26, 1957, when Mayor Willi Solish of Rostock solemnly broke ground at the Petersdorf building site for the overseas port to come. "In 1960, the first 10,000-ton ship will be loaded or unloaded at this point", Herr Solish promised* and he added, "but time is short. We'll make it only if all workingmen pitch in with all their might."

When the time came to build the new East Mole, the SED "activists" launched another of their "Socialist competition" schemes familiar in Communist economics since the early days of the Russan Revolution. For construction of the breakwater (length: 530 meters) and of the new harbor entrance, a total of 55,000 tons of rocks and stones were required. To gather this building material, free of charge, the Party mobil-

---

*This promise was kept. On May 1st, 1960, the unloading of the 10,000-ton (dwt) freighter *Schwerin* took place at the half-finished pier, giving rise to great celebrations.

ized thousands of youngsters — some, like the "Thälmann pioneers" enlisted voluntarily, while others, indeed entire school groups, were drafted — who picked up millions of ordinary field stones all over the country and loaded them aboard freight trains and barges for transportation to Warnemünde.

For all the deadly earnestness with which the organizers tackled this campaign, they could not prevent it from becoming the target of countless anti-Communist jokes. For instance, Swedish tourists visiting or passing through Rostock in 1958 made a practice of carrying pebbles to the East German customs officials as their contribution to construction of the East Mole!

Well, by hook or by crook the big breakwater was built and by July 11, 1958, this part of the job was finished. Next, on the occasion of the 9th anniversary of the DDR, October 7, 1958, the opening of the new channel gave cause to boisterous celebrations, although in fact the perforation was not completed until November 16 of that year. It was announced that 3,200,-000 cubic meters of earth and sand had been cleared away to create the passage.

In the meantime, work on the harbor installations of the new port area had progressed, too. Originally, construction of three harbor basins had been contemplated, but later their number was reduced to two. They were to be of equal size and shape and destined one for handling general cargo, the other for bulk cargo. Each was to have a quay length of 1,500 meters and a width of 180 meters. When completed, the two basins are expected to have a combined capacity of handling 16 million tons of goods annually.

In addition, a separate "oil port" designed initially for an annual capacity of one million tons — later to be increased to two and eventually to six million — was to be built at a point about one kilometer east of the main harbor.

An altogether new network of railroad tracks and sidings

is to connect the oil port with the main harbor and both with
the so-called "Eisenbahnmagistrale" (railroad trunkline) Ros-
tock-Berlin. The latter, still in the stage of construction, is a
new alternative, to the old railroad line running from Rostock
to Berlin by way of Güstrow, Malchin and Neubrandenburg,
which has been operating on a single track since the end of
the war.

Considerable mystery surrounds at this time the question of
how far advanced the new trunkline is, whether it will have
two tracks and can be completed on time. Conflicting reports
on this subject have appeared in the East and West German
papers, and it is hard to clear up the confusion at this stage.

Much of the same kind of mystery prevails regarding the
system of inland waterways in the making or planned. These,
it is agreed, will have to take the brunt of the huge amount of
cargo that is destined eventually to transit through Rostock,
since rail facilities will be inadequate in any event.

Originally, it was proposed to link the new overseas port
to the Elbe River at or near Wittenberge by means of a canal
designed to make good use of the intermediate group of lakes
known as the "Mecklenburgische Seenplatte". The idea itself
is at least 50 years old, but has been shelved, time and again,
on account of the nearly insuperable technical difficulties involved. For the considerable differences in altitude would
make necessary the installation of so many sluices that the
cost would be prohibitive, experts hold.

After announcing in 1958 with great fanfare that the controversial canal would be built regardless, the East German
planners quietly dropped this scheme the following year. As
an alternative, they hit upon the idea of digging an east-west
canal, running close to the coastline and connecting Rostock
with the Oder estuary by way of the large lagoon known as
"Saaler (Ribnitzer) Bodden" and thence through the Strela
Sound. Then, however, West German papers reported that

this project had run into an unforeseen snag: opposition from Poland, which controls the Oder estuary and would seem to look upon the Rostock venture with a somewhat jaundiced eye, since it is sure to draw away business from Stettin as well as from Hamburg.

One thing is sure, though: a practicable water connection to one or the other of these two great rivers will have to be found to ensure successful operation of the overseas port. For, not only are rail and road connections insufficient — even though a new autobahn linking Rostock to Berlin is also in the making — but transportation costs overland would be too high to make the whole thing a profitable venture. Even with the well-known tendency of Communist regimes to discount the cost factor where political and strategic considerations are paramount, it is doubtful that the Rostock project would have been undertaken if no solution of the waterway problem were in sight — as the West German papers claim, perhaps through an excess of wishful thinking.

In Hamburg, which stands to be the principal loser if the Rostock scheme turns out to be a success, the present inclination is not to take too seriously the competitive threat of his "Harbor Without Hinterland". However, only the future can tell whether the East or the West Germans' optimism concerning the prospects of Rostock is better warranted.

In the first stage of construction, completed by the end of April, 1960, the overseas port is expected to handle about two million tons of cargo, including shipments to and from the old port of Rostock (which in 1958 recorded 901,000 tons — 107,800 tons less than in 1957). Thereafter, the following target figures have been set: 1961 — 2.8 million tons; 1962 — 3.7; 1963 — 4.6; 1964 — 6.1; 1965 — 6.9; 1967 — 15.0 million tons.

In the second stage, the emphasis will be on completing the oil port with its projected short pipeline leading to a big tank farm. In the same period, ending in 1964, the new harbor terminal is to be built and the autobahn connection is to be initiated.

The third stage of construction, ending in 1969, provides for the enlargement and improvement of all existing facilities, the deepening of the channel to a depth of 12 meters and possibly the addition of a third harbor basin.

One important side-effect of this development was to weld the two towns of Rostock and Warnemünde closely together into one large shipping and industrial center including two big shipyards, important metalworking industries (at Rostock), fish-processing plants, and a university (at Rostock) with a major nautical and shipbuilding division.

This, then, was the background for my visit to Rostock. Now for a first-hand account of my impressions and of the progress achieved so far.

To begin with, a few remarks about Rostock itself. The old Hanseatic town, in the past more renowned for its university and its role as market place for a rich agricultural region than for its shipping activities, has made a remarkable comeback in recent years. Fearfully ravaged in the last war, the city has been almost completely rebuilt, mostly in the traditional representative style of Baltic Sea cities. In the earlier phase of reconstruction, however, there have been some questionable encroachments of the architectural "cheesecake" type so noteworthy on East Berlin's Stalinallee. This period of "Hanseatic stalinism", as it has been called by West German critics, produced some of the richly ornamental housefronts in the city center, especially on "Lange Strasse" or Long Street. Current building features simplicity and functionalism rather than showy ornaments.

On the whole, Rostock has done a very creditable job of reconstruction. Its public buildings, apartment houses and stores compare favorably with most other large cities in the DDR (with a present population of 155,351 it ranks eighth in the country). A brand new housing project, Reutershagen, is designed to provide Rostock's seafaring citizens with comfortable quarters in suburban surroundings; row upon row of unassuming but bright and airy apartment houses greet the eye as one drives past.

The Overseas Port

In the first place, it was not easy to gain access to the hermetically sealed-off and heavily guarded harbor area. Although my East German guide was carrying with him a pass signed, from what I gathered, by a high official of the Foreign Ministry, this magical paper did not in this case produce – the instantaneous open-sesame effect. Indeed, it was not until after the pass had been sent on, by the officer in charge of the armed guards at the gate, to the Administration Building, and had been stamped and countersigned half a dozen times, that our little party was finally admitted to the hallowed precincts.

A walk around the harbor, under the watchful eye of a high port official, showed that of the two basins under construction in what is called the "Handelshafen" or trade port, the one marked "B" was half-finished and bustling with activity, while "A" was still being dredged.

The inner portion of Basin "B" — representing about one-half of the total length planned — was virtually completed and in full operation; it can accommodate ships with drafts up to 28.5 feet, and is able to handle four ships of up to 10,000 tons at a time. In addition, there are two mooring places where other ships can await their turn at handling.

The main quay has a length of about 600 yards and is to be extended to 1,320 yards by the end of this year; it is equipped with 12 powerful cranes and one huge lifting apparatus called a crane-bridge ("Kranbrücke"). The wharf sheds have a total length of 385 yards and are 66 yards wide.

On the opposite quay, which is reserved for the loading and unloading of bulk goods, I noticed four tremendous "crane-bridges", each weighing 800 tons. This quay has been in operation since July 1, 1960, two months after the formal inauguration of the Overseas Port.

The day I visited there, the basin was filled to capacity. Among the five ships present, two large grey-hulled vessels of striking appearance, with trim lines and spick-and-span whitewashed super-structure, caught my eye. They were the *Karl-Marx-Stadt* and *Schwerin*, two of the latest 10,000-tonners built at the Warnow Shipyard. The former had just returned from a trip to China, the other from Cuba (where she had been during the abortive invasion attempt by Castro's foes).

Speaking of Cuba, I picked up another interesting item. On the spacious wharf platform behind the sheds, 90 brand-new tractors were arrayed, ready for shipment. I asked the port official who showed us around where they were going.

"To Cuba", he replied without a moment's hesitation.

"Oh, I thought Castro is getting his tractors from us," I said. (At that time it looked as though the tractor-for-prisoners deal would go through.)

"Well, I guess he needs still more", the official smiled back.

The only portion of the harbor area I was not allowed to inspect was the so-called "oil port" in the making (as distinct from the "trade port"). It is being built by Russian engineers according to entirely new and apparently secret principles, and has therefore been declared a "Sperrgebiet": out of bounds to all but the most highly qualified visitors. When finished, in 1963, the oil port will have facilities for unloading two tankers simultaneously. One pier was recently completed and is in operation (the silhouette of a Soviet tanker being unloaded there could be seen from afar).

In conclusion, this significant remark by the accompanying port official: "Of the 400 longshoremen presently employed here, about 90% had never before even seen, let alone worked in, a harbor."

21

Shipyards and
Shipbuilding in
East Germany

Before World War II, there existed along the vast stretch
of Baltic shoreline now controlled by the DDR only one major
shipyard, the Neptun-Werft of Rostock, which accounted for
about 4% of total German shipbuilding. Today, by contrast,
five large shipyards are in operation in the same area, which
together turn out about 25% of all the ships built in the two
Germanies. Persons employed in river yards and other establishments building small boats total to approximately 50,000
shipyard workers in this territory, or ten times as many as before the last war.

These figures reveal graphically an economic revolution
that has received all too little attention abroad: the fact that
shipbuilding, in a matter of a few years, has become a major
industry in Eastern Germany, and one with the highest priority rating after the basic brown coal and steel industries.

With an area of 1,119,000 square meters, the new Warnow-
Werft, located in the former resort of Warnemünde, at the mouth
of the river Warnow, is at present the biggest shipyard in the
DDR. It has been practically built from scratch since 1947,
when the then Soviet commander in Eastern Germany, Gen-

eral Chuikov, ordered the shipyard to be built on the site formerly occupied by the Arado Aircraft Works.

From afar the Warnow Shipyard attracts attention by its
imposing "Kabelkrananlage" (cable-crane-installation). The
huge structure, about 200 feet high and with an overall length
of almost 1,000 feet, is a maze of steel girders and cable lines
that dominates the countryside for miles. Twenty-four sturdy
rollers suspended on strong overhead cables convey the finished parts and other building materials from the assembly
plant to the four slipways where the ships are put together.
The covered hall of the assembly plant, where the individual
sections of a ship are welded together, is claimed to be the
largest of its kind in Europe; it is about 220 yards long and 110
yards wide.

When I visited the place, one freighter of 13,500 deadweight
tons, one of 10,000 tons, and two coal-and-ore carriers of 9,500
tons each were being built on the four slipways. The two last-
named ships had been earmarked for delivery to the Soviet
Union, which, along with other Soviet Bloc countries, still
takes the lion's share of East German shipyard production. It
is not a one-way affair, though. In return, Soviet shipyards
supply the DDR with tankers, a type of vessel not built at all
in that country. (In June and July 1961, for example, the 10,-
000-ton tankers *Boehlen* and *Zeitz*, both destined for the DDR,
were launched at the Admiralty Shipyard in Leningrad.)

Since 1952, when serial production of new seagoing ships
got under way at the Warnow Shipyard (before, the yard had
been mainly used for the conversion or repair of Soviet vessels), a total of 32 freighters aggregating 30,000 gross tons have
been built there, I was told. This includes 15 vessels of the
10,000-ton class known as "Städteklasse", because each of
those ships — insofar as they were earmarked for the DDR
merchant fleet rather than for export — bears the name of a
major East German city.

Even in the opinion of West German experts, these sleek and modern ships which have a speed of 16.5 knots and which can accommodate 12 passengers in addition to their crew of 56, represent, in spite of certain technical shortcomings, a remarkable achievement which is the more impressive as the Warnow-Werft has been in existence for such a short time only.

Here is an interesting detail I learned in passing: two of the large freighters built by the Warnow Shipyard were sold to Red China, but they are now sailing under the flags of Poland and Czechoslovakia, respectively, in order to be able to navigate undisturbed through the Strait of Formosa. One of the 10,000-tonners was earmarked for Cuba; baptized *Sierra Madre*, it was delivered to that country on December 17, 1961.

In addition to the four building slips of the cable-crane-installation, the Warnow Shipyard recently acquired, for repair purposes, a large modern floating drydock. Built by West Germany's "Gutehoffnungshütte", this drydock was delivered in December 1960; it is at present moored in a basin just outside the shipyard area proper. At a neighboring repair dock, the 23,000-ton Soviet whaling ship (floating factory) *Yuri Dolgoruky* (formerly the German liner *Hamburg*) was undergoing inspection; the vessel, converted at the Warnow Yard, had been delivered to the Soviet Union in 1960. In another dock area, I watched the Warnow-built 13,500-ton *Lübbenau*, presently the largest vessel of the state-run "Deutsche Seerederei," East Germany's principal shipping company, being outfitted. Other vessels recently launched and now being outfitted in this section of the yard included three ore-freighters ranging in size from 7,500 to 9,500 tons that are to be delivered to the Soviet Union.

From 1946 to date, I learned, more than 170 million marks have been invested in the Warnow Shipyard, which currently employs a staff of about 7,000 (5,000 thereof in production).

It is in every respect a young outfit, for the average age of the shipyard workers is only 29 years; the managing director of the enterprise, Gerhard Zimmermann, boasts the ripe old age of 35.

The old-established Neptun-Werft at Rostock (founded in 1851) has been considerably enlarged and modernized in the past few years; it now employs about 6,500 people. Although this shipyard since 1959 has undertaken the construction of 10,000-ton freighters, three of which are to be built by 1965, it still serves primarily as a repair yard and also turns out specialized ships such as the exploration vessel *Lomonossov*, built for Soviet account and used for the purposes of the Geophysical Year, as well as the *Meteor*, destined for scientific expeditions under the flag of the DDR, and the new, big ferry *Sassnitz*. This shipyard also builds trawlers, towboats, tugs, fireboats and other small craft, as well as small ore-carriers of 760 dwt. each. Interestingly, the Neptun-Werft at present is also engaged in building a series of six small motorships for a *West* German shipping company in Hamburg, the first of which was delivered early in 1959.

Currently the second-largest East German shipyard is the Mathias-Thesen-Werft of Wismar, which also employs 7,000 persons. This again is a new and modern yard, built from scratch in the years 1946-50. In addition to four launching slips, it has a dry dock capable of accommodating vessels up to 25,000 gross tons in size.

Established by order of the Soviet Military Government, the Mathias-Thesen-Werft, in its first years of existence, was used to repair and convert former German merchant ships and naval craft destined to be turned over to the Russians on reparations account. In this period, it also produced icebreakers for Soviet Russia. Since July 1953, some 20 small passenger ships have been built there for Soviet account; this type of vessel, 96 meters long and built solely of light metals above the water-line, is destined for inland navigation. Among other craft on the 1960-65 construction program are ten large fishing and fish-processing vessels, one floating factory for whaling (for Soviet account), one cruise ship, and a number of medium-sized combined cargo and passenger vessels.

Third in size is the Volkswerft (People's Shipyard) Stralsund, where 5,000 workers are employed. This shipyard is located on the Strela Sound in the vicinity of the Rügendamm which links the island of Rügen with the Pomeranian mainland and is on the site of a former experimental station operated in World War II by the German Navy. The Volkswerft Stralsund, too, was built by order of the Soviet authorities, beginning in October 1946.

The Volkswerft builds exclusively trawlers and other fishing vessels, mostly for domestic and Soviet account; 12 of these craft have recently been exported to Iceland.

Smallest of the East German shipyards that build seagoing vessels is the Peene-Werft of Wolgast, a small town about 31 miles southeast of Stralsund, which employs 1,500 people. This yard produces primarily small and medium-sized motorships for coastal traffic, as well as for trans-Baltic service to the Scandinavian countries.

In addition to these major shipyards, there are nine fairly large river yards along the Elbe, Havel and Oder rivers, as well as a number of small boat-building enterprises. Some of the latter are still privately owned, while all the major yards are state property.

In the course of the First Five-Year-Plan (1951-55), the East German shipyards turned out a total of 1,344 ships, aggregating 324,000 gross tons; during the second, ending in 1960, they delivered a total of about 626,000 gross tons.

While the East German shipyards are generally modern

and well equipped, production is frequently hampered by shortages of specific items and the failure of subcontractors to effect deliveries on schedule. Diesel engines, ships' pumps, electrical equipment and wireless apparatus have been often mentioned in the East German press as "bottlenecks" in shipbuilding.

In spite of these difficulties, East German shipbuilding, and shipping in 1961, chalked up another big advance. A total of fourteen new vessels were put in service during that year by the "Deutsche Seereederi," bringing the total DDR fleet to 61 ships with an aggregate tonnage of 300,000 deadweight tons.

Part 4

German Duel for Africa

22

The Germans in Africa:
To the Natives,
They Look Alike

"Germans against Germans in Africa! . . . " "The German civil war in the jungle has begun . . ." These scary phrases appeared on September 18, 1960, in the most widely read of all West German newspapers, the *Bild* of Hamburg (Sunday edition). As is usual with that sensation-mongering sheet, the contents of the story were not quite as startling as the headlines and bold-type catchwords, but they were nevertheless interesting.

The German Trade Union Federation or DGB (Deutscher Gewerkschaftsbund), it appears, had decided to meet the challenge of African labor's Communist penetration by its East German counterpart, the FDGB (Freier Deutscher Gewerkschaftsbund). West Germany's DGB, it should be added, is strongly influenced by the Social-Democratic Party (SPD), while the East German FDGB is completely under the thumb of the "Socialist Unity Party" (SED), in other words, the Communists.

It had been known for some time that the FDGB had been

picked by the East German policy-makers as the most effective spearhead of Communist penetration into the dark Continent. In many of the young states of Africa, trade unionism is one of the most potent, if not *the* most potent of social forces, and its political position has not yet, as a rule, crystallized; it is therefore susceptible to aggressive influences from abroad.

"For months, the emissaries of Pankow, misusing the good name of Germany, have been creating mischief in the Dark Continent", one read in *Bild*, "but now the DGB is going to strike back. By arrangement with the International Federation of Free Trade Unions in Brussels, the DGB will send its own representatives to Africa ..."

The Hamburg paper then quoted the "Africa expert" of the DGB, Herbert A. Tulatz, as saying: "The Communist agents deliberately keep silent about their Soviet zone origins. Many Africans, of course, are not aware of Germany's division. Frequently on my trip through Africa, I was asked by somebody: "When you get back home, please give my best regards to your colleague, Herr X, in Leipzig".

A good many other West Germans in Africa (and not there alone) have had similar experiences. The natives, even if by chance they have heard of the 16-year-old division of Germany into rival and inimical halves, for the most part can't tell the difference between one German and another. To them, Hamburg, Munich, Leipzig, Magdeburg, etc., are cities of one country. The visitors from those places look alike, they speak the same language, and quite often they offer almost identical goods and services. That they are politically poles apart is not immediately apparent and besides, most Africans couldn't care less. What they are interested in is trade, financing, educational facilities and technical assistance — not ideologies or political associations. And in the East-West conflict, they would much rather stay on the sidelines, anyway.

The East Germans' propaganda drive in Africa is of comparatively recent date. Until the middle fifties, the Pankow Government showed little interest in African affairs. From 1956 on, however, the "Africa bureaus" and "Africa institutes" suddenly began to sprout all over the DDR. African students, lured by handsome scholarships, flocked by the hundreds to East German institutions of higher learning. At the same time, trade and cultural delegations from the DDR began to descend en masse on the newly emanicipated countries of the Dark Continent. The advent to independence of each new state was watched closely by the East German Government, and preparations were made well in advance of each such event to make the most, politically as well as commercially, of the new opportunity.

One may take it for granted that the well-planned and efficiently organized invasion of the Black Continent by the "Red Africa Corps" composed of Communist-minded intellectuals, unionists, traders and technicians was not entirely sparked by East German initiative alone. The DDR is an all-out Soviet satellite, much more so than, say, Poland or even Czechoslovakia. Whatever it does, in any field of endeavor, is closely coordinated with Moscow's aims and integrated into its planning. Undoubtedly, therefore, it was the Kremlin that assigned to the East Germans a leading role in the struggle for the black man's mind.

There was shrewd calculation behind this move, too. The Germans, regardless of whether they hail from the western or the eastern portion of the country, are popular in Africa as well as in the adjoining Near East. Having lost their own colonies more than forty years ago, the Germans, in those parts, are looked upon as the one important branch of the white race that is untainted by the curse of colonialism. Even in those territories like Tanganyika and Togo, where memories of the German overlords of the time before World War I still linger, the natives nowadays remember the blessings of efficient ad-

ministration and good education rather than the evils of colonial exploitation and repression of which the Germans in
those days were guilty just as much as any other European
power in Africa.

The high prestige which the Germans enjoy both among
the Arabs and in Black Africa is due to a peculiar combination
of diverse elements, not all of which are praiseworthy. The
well-known German author Peter Grubbe, who has written a
number of informative books about Africa and Asia, dealt
with this curious subject in an enlightening article entitled
"Deutsche Legende in Afrika" (The German Legend in Africa), which appeared in *Die Welt* of Hamburg on March 11,
1960.

"Everywhere in Africa, from Cairo to Capetown, from Mom-
basa to Leopoldville, it's the same story", Herr Grubbe wrote.
"The German traveling through Africa these days encounters
everywhere admiration, recognition, affection, even something
approaching veneration. One hears remarks such as these: 'The
Germans are a wonderful people. They are going to help us.
And they are so clever. You can trust the Germans. Oh, you
are German? I'm so glad to meet you. Tell me all about your
country, which we all admire so much over here . . .' "

Trying to analyze the sources of these feelings, the German
author came up with some surprising conclusions. "The reasons why people admire the Germans and speak so well of
them, are many and varied", he wrote. "In Tanganyika (formerly German East Africa), people fondly recall General Let-
tow-Vorbeck; in the Cameroons, it's the German administration before the First World War. In Libya, Field Marshal Rommel remains unforgotten and, in Egypt, Hitler's deeds are
praised. In the Sudan, an eminent German ambassador and
the accomplishments of two German industrial concerns give
rise to feelings of admiration, while in the Belgian Congo Germany is praised for not possessing any colonies."

Herr Grubbe himself was surprised at this motley of African reasons for loving Germany: "That present-day Germany has no colonies, is our good fortune, not our merit . . . Rommel was a brave soldier and a fine general . . . who led a chivalrous army . . . but, what Africa needs today is good political leaders rather than good soldiers . . ."

As regards Hitler, the author admits in shame and disgust, the main reason why the Arabs love the Germans is because they murdered so many Jews. "Why, Hitler did a splendid job on the Jews, you Germans are great guys", Herr Grubbe quotes some of his Arab friends as telling him. Summing up, he finds that the German prestige in Africa is largely based on a myth, rather than on anything the Federal Republic has done since it came into being 11 years ago for Black Africa or for the Arabs.

Whatever the true nature of the German heritage may be, it is clear from the observations of Peter Grubbe — which are supported by those of other seasoned journalists as well as parliamentarians who recently toured Africa — that German prestige in the area is high. And the East German Communists profit from this state of affairs as much as the representatives of the Federal Republic.

On the other hand, the East Germans have a number of distinct propaganda advantages over their Western competitors. For one thing, they usually are able to offer better terms for two-way trade. Invariably, as soon as a new African state has been proclaimed independent, the East Berlin Government's first move is to send a trade mission there. Now, while the DDR can offer to the underdeveloped nations much the same kind of technical assistance as they might get from Western Germany — plant installations, heavy machinery, consulting engineers, etc. — it is in a much better position for barter arrangements than the Federal Republic is.

Indeed, what most African nations would like to sell in exchange for the capital goods and consumer wares they so urgently need is agricultural products and minerals that are a glut on the world market — bananas, cocoa, coffee, sugar, rubber, ores, oil, cotton. The Bonn Government, which cannot force West German consumers to buy what they don't want, thus finds itself at a disadvantage in trading, while Eastern Germany, which is constantly beset by food scarcities, and where all trade is handled by government agencies, has no qualms about contracting for large deliveries of agricultural produce from Africa.

In propaganda, too, the East Germans have the bigger guns on their side. By pointing to NATO, they can link the Bonn Government to the favorite African (and Arab) bugaboos of "imperialism" and "colonialism". For instance, early in 1960, East German propagandists throughout northern and central Africa circulated the unproved allegation that West Germany had helped France manufacture the "Sahara-bomb". Among the Arabs, anti-Israeli feelings are also played upon, for the Bonn Government is doing its best to make amends for the crimes of the Third Reich by paying reparations to Israel, while the DDR has never done anything for that country.

The West Germans are trying to counter this propaganda offensive by pointing to the evils of Communism. This is a blunt weapon, for Communism means nothing to Africans, who have not experienced it and who think in terms of food and clothing rather than of ideologies and political freedom. Nor does it do much good to preach democracy among people who are not yet mature enough to grasp its true meaning and who could hardly tell the difference from "people's democracy", anyway.

23

Prime Object of
The Tug-of-War:
The Intelligentsia

Africa, where illiteracy is still rife and that most dangerous thing, "a little learning", is rampant in many parts, holds the educated man in high regard. According to Herbert Tulatz, "any African who has spent in Europe as little as four months as a student is regarded back home as an expert and qualifies for the highest positions."

Both sides in the German duel for Africa are well aware of this and are doing their utmost to draw the budding intelligentsia of the new African states into their camp. Never before in history has any group of people been so eagerly wooed as the would-be African student today. He has before him a practically unlimited choice of scholarships and opportunities for learning the easy way. He can go to the United States as a guest of the Kennedy Foundation or he can get his free tuition, board and lodging in Moscow, Prague, Warsaw or Budapest. In Germany, he can pick practically any university on either side of the demarcation line and get all he wants free for the asking.

In lavishing this hospitality on black students, the DDR appears to have stolen a march on the Federal Republic. There, the drive for African student enrollment at the badly overcrowded universities is only now getting under way; while Leipzig, Dresden, Jena, Rostock and other centers of higher learning in East Germany have been filled with African students for years. Out of a total student body of 35,000 in 1960, at the six universities of the DDR, some 2,000 were foreigners. While in previous years students from the Soviet bloc countries predominated among the alien students, African, Asian and Latin American nationals have been increasingly in evidence in the past year or so.

A writer in *Die Welt* of August 11, 1960, told of his experiences in interviewing some of these black-babes-in-the-redwood. He was startled by their political naivité and the way they had been thoroughly indoctrinated after a short stay only in East Germany. What he heard from their lips ran about like this: "The DDR is the best country under the sun. Here, simple workers drive SIM-sedans (a Soviet make of car), they dine in the plushest hotels and feast on Russian caviar and champagne. The poor people have been housed in the manors of the rich. The government has given factories and rural estates to the poor. All simple people become professors, managers and ministers."

The core of this campaign to win the hearts and minds of young Africans is, of course, Moscow. There, the "Africa Institute" of the Soviet Academy of Sciences is the principal center of research and propaganda activities aimed at the Dark Continent; it is headed by Professor Ivan Potekhin who is rated as the Soviet Union's top expert on African affairs. The membership of the Institute includes many young scholars from various African nations.

A full-fledged "Africa Institute" was also opened, in the early fall of 1960, at the University of Leipzig. Its primary purpose is to train East German diplomats and trade representatives for service in Africa. The faculty of the Institute is to be expanded in the coming years to include 20 historians, 24 economists, 10 jurists, 4 art historians and 2 philosophers.

In Leipzig, capital of the East German book trade, a new state-owned publishing house, "VEB Edition Leipzig", was organized early in September 1960 for the specific purpose of publishing propagandistic books aimed at the young African states.

Also in Leipzig, there is an FDGB propaganda institute whose principal function it is to attract African union leaders and to provide them with a "primer on socialism", printed in English and French; it is distributed to all comers free of charge. Leipzig thus has emerged as the capital of the East German propaganda drive aimed at Africa.

In East Berlin, on July 23, 1960, a "Committee for Solidarity with the Nations of Africa" was set up. According to East German press reports delegates from 14 African countries attended the inaugural ceremonies in which some 50 prominent personalities of the DDR also took part.

Broadcasting also plays an important part in the Soviet Bloc's master plan for the ideological conquest of Africa. Radio Moscow has been beaming special programs to that continent for several years; a novelty is a course in the Russian language that was added in the fall of 1960. More recently, an East Berlin transmitter also has begun short-wave broadcasts in French and English for African consumption.

In its endeavor to capture political footholds in Africa, the Soviet Bloc, for the time being, is playing down party-line ideology. Emissaries to the Dark Continent seldom profess to be Communist party members. As a rule, they affect to be artists, unionists, traders, parliamentarians and members of "anti-Fascist" resistance groups, noted the *Münchner Merkur* on March 8, 1960, in a survey entitled "Pankow in Africa".

West Germany is now making a big effort to draw away some of the African intelligentsia that have been flocking to East Germany in the past few years. The West German press, on September 22, 1960, gave a big play to the story of three African students who had publicly disavowed their Soviet teachers ("We left Moscow in disgust ... others will do so, too"), adding that the young men now would enroll at West German universities. Austria, too, is lending a helping hand in this struggle for the Black Continent's intellectual elite. An "Afro-Asian Institute" has recently been opened in Vienna for the purpose of introducing students from those continents to Western civilization and the Western way of life.

A dispatch from Bonn published in"The Christian Science Monitor"of April 8, 1961, gave these additional details of the German propaganda war raging over Africa:

"East German Communist propagandists nowadays are exerting strenuous efforts to prove to the newly independent states of Africa and Asia that "neocolonialism" is their greatest enemy — and that the (West) German Federal Republic is one of the strongest leaders of neocolonialism.

"This is stressed in a congress now in progress in Leipzig to which special guests from Africa, Asia, and South America have been invited. The theme of the congress is the 'problems of neocolonialism and the policy of both German states toward the national liberation struggle of people.'

"What stands out in reports of the first few days of the meeting is the obvious realization that the Communists cannot hope for a long time to surpass the Western world's aid to these developing countries and that therefore the Communists must do all possible to misrepresent it.

"Since the (West) German Federal Republic itself has not had any colonies since the end of World War I, it is only by representing such aid as 'neocolonialism' can the Communists hope to make any headway with their propaganda against the Bonn government.

"East German Foreign Minister Lothar Bolz told the congress that the time has come to tear off the mask of the modern 'colonial policy of the West German militarists.' He recommended that the newly independent states establish diplomatic relations with East Germany and pointed out that one-sided recognition of the 'other German state' was helping 'militarism' and was contrary to the concepts of neutrality, non-interference, and peaceful coexistence . . . .

"Communist propaganda organizations also distributed scores of books, pamphlets, and the like, to the congress, which sought to prove that the federated republic was a 'robber in the garb of benefactor.'

"Specially attacked in a book entitled 'Bonn — African Peoples' Enemy' was Dr. Eugen Gerstenmaier, speaker of the Bundestag (lower house), who has made a number of trips to Africa in recent years. He was represented as a disguised Nazi and imperialist. . . ."

In the first half of 1962, the East-West German struggle for superior influence in Africa gathered further momentum. On the West German side, this propaganda drive was highlighted by an eleven-day tour of West African countries (Liberia, Guinea and Senegal) which the President of the Federal Republic, Heinrich Lübke, undertook in January, accompanied by Foreign Minister Gerhard Schröder.

Before taking off from Dakar airport, on January 21, for the return trip to Bonn, President Lübke remarked: "The German people have great opportunities in Africa, and they have many sincere friends there."

The East Germans think so, too. At the Leipzig Spring Fair, in March 1962, a recently organized "German-African Society" played host to a select group of African politicians, businessmen and trade union leaders from various countries.

In his formal address to the dark-hued guests, the president of the Society, Gerald Goetting, claimed that the "imperialists" in Washington, London and Bonn had done everything in their power to keep the African visitors away from the Leipzig Fair,but the "true friend of the black man," the DDR, had managed to overcome these obstacles.

At the same time it was learned that the East German Trade Union Federation (FDGB) in 1961 had spent 2,300,000 marks in support of left-wing native movements, mainly in Algeria, Angola, the Congo and South Africa. Announcing these "gifts of solidarity," the FDGB issued an "African Declaration" that said, among other things: "Our hearts beat together with your hearts for the freedom of Africa from Algier to the Cape."

24

Gifts From All Comers
Gladly Accepted

Among the many interesting, and frequently dramatic, episodes to which this all-German tug-of-war for African sympathies has given rise, three in particular deserve to be treated in some detail, not only because the countries involved — Egypt, Guinea and Ghana — are among the most important in Africa, but also because of the diplomatic complications involved.

Probably the most noteworthy case in point is that of Egypt, alias the United Arab Republic. To date, President Nasser has been completely successful in balancing his eagerness to take economic and military (atomic development, rocketry) aid from West Germany against his perfect willingness to accept such aid from the DDR also.

This balancing act began some four years ago and is still going strong in mid-1962. Let us have a good look at this remarkable tight-rope performance.

"We have concluded an agreement for a loan of L.E.* 44 millions from West Germany. By virtue of this agreement,

---

*L. E. = the Egyptian pound, nominally worth U.S. $2.87.

West Germany will supply capital goods worth L.E. 44 millions required for the five-year industrial plan.

"We also concluded an agreement with East Germany for a loan of L.E. 7,500,000, for financing these projects; and concluded another agreement with Japan for a loan of L.E. 30 millions for the industrialization scheme . . ."

Thus spoke Gamal Abdel Nasser, President of the United Arab Republic, in an address to the General Cooperatives' Conference, held at the Ceremonial Hall of Cairo University, on November 27, 1958.

A short time earlier, one could read in the *Egyptian Economic and Political Review* (which, like all other newspapers and magazines in the U.A.R., is tightly controlled by the Government) this candid commentary:

"President Nasser's visit to Moscow will make a happy period in Egypt's international relations, for in addition to Russian friendship, the day of his arrival in Moscow was chosen by Mr. Dulles to make his announcement of an unfreezing of funds in the U.S.A. In addition, a few days later at about the time the President was receiving a sword on board the Soviet heavy cruiser *Kutusov*, in the Black Sea, Dr. Erhard was signing a loan to Egypt of some 40 million marks."

These two utterances from authoritative Egyptian sources are typical of the unconcerned, gladhanded way the U.A.R. has been (and still is) accepting economic aid from all nations willing and able to provide such, regardless of political affiliations. This disarmingly frank impartiality in taking favors from all comers, whether they be Westerners or Easterners, capitalists or communists, has been most strikingly demonstrated in the case of divided Germany.

Nasser's outlook on the German problem can be summed up simply: this staunch advocate of "positive neutralism" likes to do business with the democratic West Germans as much as with the Communist-controlled East Germans; and, for good measure, he also shelters (and even coddles) in his country a large number of Nazi Germans, relics of the Third Reich as well as a few latecomers who have just shaken the dust of the Federal Republic off their nimble feet.

Since the Germans, among themselves, do not exhibit quite such brotherly feelings, this bighearted Egyptian policy has given rise to some friction and there have been some pointed hints that Nasser better make up his mind on which shoulder he wants to carry his German water. So far, he apparently hasn't decided, or else he intends to carry on with all three varieties of Germans as before, regardless of consequence.

This peculiar situation reached a climax about the turn of the year 1958-59,when West German and East German delegations, awaiting their turn to be received at the Presidential Palace in Cairo, practically stepped on each other's toes. To say nothing about the American, British, French, Italian and Japanese negotiators who at the same time were crowding Nasser's ante-chamber, all eager to help make Egypt into a powerful industrial nation, as are the Russians for that matter.

The uneasy 1958 procession of German gift-bearers to Cairo began on November 1st, when Dr. Hans Christoph Seebohm, West German Minister of Transportation, flew to Cairo on the first non-stop airplane service inaugurated by the Lufthansa. It was the first official visit paid to Egypt since the end of the war by any member of the Bonn Government. Seebohm was accompanied on this trip by a large delegation of German officials, businessmen — in particular the industrial magnate Ernst von Siemens — and various members of the Bundestag. On November 8, Seebohm was received by President Nasser.

Upon his return to Germany, at the end of a ten-day stay in Egypt, Seebohm was quoted as saying that he had found Nasser to be "a modest, retiring man with nothing of the dictator about him", whose principal problem was finding food and work for his people. He added that, to his mind, the Arabs were not anti-Semitic, although they were opposed to the state of Israel. The Minister expressed the opinion that West Germany should help Egypt even more than in the past and should in particular help train technicians for Egypt's modernization plans.

Dr. Seebohm announced after his return to Germany that his colleague in the Bonn Government, Professor Ludwig Erhard, Minister of Economic Affairs, was also planning a visit to Cairo, early in 1959. This visit, however, did not take place until a year later, presumably because of the coolness in German-Egyptian relations that developed about the turn of the year.

Next, a three-man mission of West German technical experts, headed by Dr. Hans Kuntze, a member of the board of the German Association for Aid to the Underdeveloped Countries, arrived in Cairo on November 25 for talks with Egyptian officials in connection with an agreement on technical assistance signed at Bonn on May 7, 1958. Main purpose of this visit was for the Germans to study methods for concentrating and utilizing the iron and manganese deposits that have recently been found in the Kosseir area and in the Sinai Penisula. A few days later, a group of technicians from the Krupp Works of Essen arrived for the purpose of studying the geological and technical conditions for the establishment of a pig-iron processing plant at Suez.

In between these friendly visits from West Germany (and there were others, too, that received less public attention), the East Germans also came to Cairo to pay their respects and offer tribute to the strong man of the Orient. Naturally enough, they too, were received with open arms.

East Germany has for several years maintained in Cairo a well-staffed "trade mission," headed by Richard Gyptner, a veteran Communist. In the absence of formal diplomatic relations between the U.A.R. and the DDR — which Cairo could not risk establishing without the near-certainty of a break with Bonn — this trade mission little by little came to take on most of the functions of an unofficial embassy, complete with cultural and press attachés. The significance of this development is underlined by the fact that Herr Gyptner enjoys the personal rank of an ambassador and represents East German interests throughout the Middle East. On November 18, 1958 — barely a week after Dr. Seebohm had departed — Gyptner was granted a full-dress audience with President Nasser at the Republican (Koubbeh) Palace — the first since he had taken up his duties in Cairo.

Gyptner's reception at the Presidential Palace apparently served to pave the way for the coming of a large-sized East German trade delegation, headed by Gerhard Weiss, Deputy Minister for External Trade of the DDR, which arrived in Cairo November 25. Among the ten members of this group figured prominently the name of the head of East Germany's Central Bank. The delegation was to negotiate a new long-term commercial agreement with the U.A.R., to come into operation in 1959, and also two separate trade and payments agreements with each of the then two regions of the U.A.R.' (Egypt and Syria).

Trade-wise, East Germany for some time has been in Nasser's eyes anything but a "quantité négligable". For, the DDR in recent years has been the largest single importer of Egyptian cotton yarns and cotton goods* — and cotton still is Egypt's main export staple. About one-third of total Egyptian exports of cotton yarn is currently absorbed by East Germany. Hence, Herr Weiss received just as warm a welcome (if not a warmer one) than that which had been extended to Herr Seebohm. And the press of the U.A.R. was warned not to make

---

The Egyptian Gazette, November 26, 1958.

any nasty cracks about the "Soviet zone" or "Pankow", but to refer to the visitors as representatives of the "German Democratic Republic."

The talks between the Weiss delegation and U.A.R. officials, in particular Dr. Abdel Moneim El-Kassouni, Minister of Economic Affairs in the central government, and Mr. Hassan Abbas Zaky, Minister of Economy in the Egyptian Region, were largely concerned with implementation of an economic agreement between U.A.R. and DDR that was signed in East Berlin on August 29, 1958. Under the terms of this accord, East Germany granted to Egypt the $20,250,000 loan referred to in Nasser's speech, as quoted above. The loan was to be given in the form of long-term deliveries of complete industrial plants, industrial equipment and machine tool products.

As Herr Weiss and associates started out for Cairo by air, the municipality of East Berlin let it be known that it was donating to the Egyptians a complete mobile ambulance unit as a gesture of unselfish good will.

Although relations between U.A.R. and DDR subsequently cooled off somewhat due to recurring friction between Moscow and Cairo on the political level, trading between the two countries continued to be very active. According to *Die Welt* of Hamburg (March 25, 1959), the Soviet zone that year expected to increase its volume of trade with the U.A.R. by 25%. And an inconspicuous item published in the same paper on February 11, 1959, related: "In Cairo, citadel of Pan-Arabism, the Wartburg passenger car produced in the Soviet zone nowadays represents the make most widely used by cab drivers".

In the following years, too, Nasser continued to take from both Germanies with both hands, while maintaining an almost contemptuous show of political independence.

On January 18, 1960, on the very eve of the departure for Cairo of a large West German delegation headed by Economics Minister Prof. Ludwig Erhard, the U.A.R. Government announced that a new accord had been concluded reserving also the "second stage" of the Aswan Dam construction for the Soviet Union. This meant that the West German trip to Cairo had become purposeless for Erhard, for his group had previously been encouraged to believe that a West German participation in the Aswan project would be welcome and they were prepared to negotiate about it. Now, they realized, it would be their hated competitors in East Germany instead who would be called upon, like other Soviet satellites, to participate in this construction.

Erhard took this affront so much to heart that he fell ill in Cairo (it was a *real*, though slight, indisposition that was deliberately blown up into a diplomatic illness) and returned home prematurely on January 31st.

But again the differences between Bonn and Cairo were patched up and early in 1961 arrangements were made for a visit to Bonn by U.A.R. Vice-President Abdel Latif Mahmoud El-Boghdadi at the head of a group of economic experts. Even as the West Germans early in May were getting ready to roll out the red carpet, they learned to their dismay that East Germany had received permission to set up a consulate-general also in Damascus, capital of Syria.

Bonn was furious — and had reason to be. "Does Nasser Want To Provoke Bonn?" ran a headline in the leading economic journal *Industriekurier* of Düsseldorf on May 18. Other West German newspapers expressed similar feelings.

Now the Egyptians reacted sourly, and Cairo let it be known that the Boghdadi mission would cancel its trip to Bonn. Then the diplomatic troubleshooters once more got into the act. They again did a good job, for on June 25, 1961, the U.A.R. delegation arrived in West Germany where it stayed for three days.

Upshot of the negotiations was an accord under which Bonn promised an additional 500 million marks for the construction of an Euphrates River dam in Syria and to help finance also other projects "intended to improve the basic industrial structure of the U.A.R."

At a dinner Prof. Erhard gave on June 26 in honor of Boghdadi, the German Economics Minister hailed this agreement as "a milestone in the friendly relations between the Arab world and our country."

But the milestone didn't bring Bonn one step nearer its aim of getting the DDR diplomats out of Egypt and Syria. Not only was the East German consulate-general set up in Damascus (and maintained after Syria had broken away from the U.A.R.), but the DDR's consulate-general in Cairo was quietly converted into a full-dress diplomatic representation now headed by "Ambassador" Wolfgang Kiesewetter. (In mid-February 1962, Keisewetter was also accredited as special envoy to Ethiopia and was received by Emperor Haile Selassie in this capacity.)

Once again the Bonn-Cairo-Pankow triangle, with its possibly ominous implications especially for Israel, was highlighted on the occasion of the tenth anniversary of the Egyptian revolution. On July 21, 1962, opening day of the week-long celebration, Nasser and his top military leaders watched excitedly as four powerful single-stage rockets, each able to go as far as 400 miles, roared into the sky from a desert firing range west of Cairo. Nasser, at the time, claimed the rockets were a home-grown product, but that was true only in the sense that they had been manufactured in Egypt.

By whom? Two days later, the *Abendzeitung* of Munich let the cat out of the bag. 250 West German rocket experts ostensibly employed by a Swiss firm were working secretly for Nasser, the paper asserted. It identified the top man of the German rocket team in Egypt as Prof. Eugen Saenger of Stuttgart, a rocket expert of world-wide reputation, who a few months earlier had resigned from his post as director of the Institute of Jet Propulsion Techniques in Stuttgart. (*The New*

York Times, on August 5, 1962, confirmed this information but put a lower figure on the number of German rocket men working in Egypt. The paper stated there were "at least fifty German specialists on loan to Egypt as part of the West German aid" and reported that Saenger and three other specialists in rocketry had been paid $450,000 by the U.A.R. — evidently out of West German funds.)

On the same date that the West German *Abendzeitung* broke this sensational piece of news, the East German press carried an article by Ambassador Kiesewetter entitled "Salute to UAR National Day" from which a few quotations are in order:

"After a superficial examination you might come to the conclusion that the relations between the UAR and West Germany are excellent and that everything is running smoothly.

"Trade is, although there is a sinking tendency, extensive. But trade has been unbalanced for many years, with West Germany exporting four times what it imports from the UAR. In June 1961 West Germany promised the UAR extensive credits, although little progress has been made in the realisation so far. Without doubt, there are many contacts in the fields of culture and science.

"But all these facts cannot hide the truth that hearty relations between the two countries do not exist, for which there are several major reasons.

"The first is West Germany's NATO partnership with France. It is well known officially in Cairo that West Germany was not sparing in its financial support for France during the Algerian war. It is also a known fact that the West German Government aids in recruiting for the French Foreign Legion.

"In addition there is the West German attitude toward Israel. No one in Cairo believes that the West German Government will cease aiding this country after the end of the so-called reparations payments. Israeli efforts to become associated with the European Common Market are warmly welcomed in Bonn...

"In Cairo one understands the aims of West German imperialism. Particularly in the recent past the press has expressed displeasure with Adenauer's attitude towards the Soviet-American negotiation. On the banks of the Nile people are also interested in a relaxation of tension in Europe. It is therefore not surprising that a West German diplomat complained in Cairo that West Germany had never been subjected to so much criticism as in the recent past...

"Certainly, relations between the UAR and the DDR are different, but it is an advantage that they rest upon a clear and healthy basis.

"This basis is the mutual struggle against imperialism, the uniform opinion on many vital international questions such as the need for disarmament, for a nuclear test ban, for peaceful coexistence, for liquidation of foreign military bases and others.

"In its relations with the UAR the DDR is guided by the following principle: good and friendly cooperation with the newly independent states which have freed themselves from imperialist and colonial suppression.

"Since the conclusion of the first trade agreement of March 1953 relations have continuously improved. Today the DDR ranks seventh amongst the UAR's trading partners. As part of the trade agreement the DDR will deliver complete factories to the UAR, especially textile plants.

"Friendly contacts are also developing in the fields of culture, the sciences and sports.

"The DDR was one of the countries which consistently supported the national independence of the Egyptian people and which condemned the imperialist aggression against Egypt. The DDR offered every possible moral and material support.

"The newspaper, *Al Ahram* quoted President Nasser on February 1st, 1957, who had said:

" '*Egypt will not forget the countries who aided us in our struggle against the forces of colonialism and will not forget the peoples who supported us in our struggle for freedom and peace, for progress and a rise in our living standard. The German Democratic Republic was a true friend to us and on several occasions proved to us its noble intentions*' . . .

"In the UAR it is well known that there are two German states with different social systems. It is also an adopted fact that the German problem can be solved only in a peaceful way, which means understanding between the two German states.

"Relations between the GDR and the UAR have expanded constantly and have become very friendly. We feel sure that these existing friendly relations between our two peoples will continue and consolidate and that they will obtain the corresponding external form.

"We wish the Government and the people of the UAR further success in the reconstruction of their country and in the realisation of their far-reaching plans."

25

Other Focal Points
Of the Struggle:
Ghana and Guinea

Ghana, first of the new crop of African nations, has been a hotbed of Communist activities ever since it gained independence in 1957. This is not to say that Ghana has become an all-out Sovet satellite or that its able leader, President Kwame Nkrumah, is a Communist — although he sometimes seems to be very anxious to accommodate the Soviet Bloc, as he did for instance in his address to the United Nations General Assembly in September, 1960. And again a year later after his return from Peking and Moscow, when he sacked practically the entire British officers' corps of the Ghanaian Army and his controlled press charged Britain with complicity in the death of U.N. Secretary General Dag Hammarskjoeld.

"The center of SED (East German) propaganda activities in the young African states is at Accra, capital of Ghana", Ulrich Rühmland wrote in a lengthy, well-documented survey of "East Zone Activities in African States" that was published in the March, 1960, issue of the distinguished foreign affairs monthly *Aussenpolitik* (Stuttgart). He added, "as is well known, Ghana was recognized by the Pankow Government within 24 hours after its declaration of independence. The Soviet zone trade delegation in Accra at present numbers no less than 20 persons".

The German author then gave these additional details, significant not only in the facts they present but in the "building Socialism" atmosphere that they convey: In September, 1959, the vice-premier of Ghana paid a visit to East Berlin for talks with the Minister of Foreign Trade in the DDR, Henrich Rau, and his deputies Eckloff and Weiss. In the course of these negotiations, the East Germans agreed to import from Ghana in 1960 an additional quota of 30,000 tons of bananas and to supply in return machinery and pharmaceutical products. A few days later, on September 20, Ghana's Secretary of State, Dowoona Hamuona, and C. G. Baah, a member of his country's parliament, had talks with Heinrich Rau concerning the admission of Ghanaian students to institutions of higher learning and specialized schools in the DDR. In mid-October 1959, a delegation of Ghanaian trade unions arrived in East Berlin to attend the fifth FDGB Convention at the Dynamo Sports Stadium. The visitors from Ghana then were shown around a number of agricultural cooperatives, the new metallurgical combine at Stalinstadt and other plants.

At Stalinstadt, Rühmland goes on to report, the head of the Ghanaian trade union delegation, Attimur, and his deputy, Addei, were lifted up by members of the "Free German Youth" organization and carried in triumph through the city. They also visited military installations and were quoted in the East German press as being "enthusiastic" about "Socialist contruction" as well as the National People's Army's "readiness for combat".

That the good relations between Ghana and the DDR have not cooled off since this promising start, is evidenced by more recent press reports. Early in March, 1960, an East German delegation headed by Deputy Trade Minister Karl Eckloff visited Ghana, while an industrial exhibition featuring progress in the DDR was shown in Accra. At the same time, Ghana's Minister of Information and Education, Baako, was visiting the Leipzig Trade Fair.

Also at the same time, a prominent West German, Premier Georg August Zinn, a Social-Democrat, was in Accra at the head of a six-man delegation from the Federal Republic that had been invited to attend the celebrations of Ghana's third anniversary as an independent state. In spite of the somewhat strained atmosphere, Ghana officials managed to keep both rival German delegations comparatively happy. In this connection, the *Ghana Times* published an obviously inspired editorial stressing that the African countries did not wish to take sides in the political and diplomatic contest between the two German governments, but that they must insist on their right to maintain good relations with both, pending reunification of Germany.

On May 11, 1960, the East German official news agency ADN reported the signing in East Berlin of a new cultural exchange agreement with Ghana. The accord, signed on behalf of the African republic by Magnus George, deputy general secretary of the Trade Union Congress of Ghana, stipulated that East Germany would increase its educational help to Ghana and would set up a "friendship center" at Accra.

Again, at the end of August, 1960, Ghana's Minister of Labor, Amoska Attah, turned up in East Berlin at the head of another delegation intent on strengthening the collaboration between the two countries, especially in economic matters.

This visit coincided with a most important development on a different front — the signing in Moscow, on August 28, of a trade and technical cooperation agreement in which the Soviet Union promised to invest 160 million rubles (45 million dollars) in the development of Ghana's mineral and industrial resources. Specifically, the two countries pledged their coop-eration in geological prospecting of Ghana's mineral wealth, in building industrial plants and power dams, in setting up model state farms and in the training of Ghanaian workers.

Whether and to what extent the Soviet Union would also participate in President Nkrumah's pet development project, the Volta Dam, was not immediately apparent. This 170 mil-lion dollars hydroelectric scheme has come to be a fair coun-terpart, at least in its international aspects, of the Aswan Dam imbroglio in Egypt. Only a few days before the Moscow agree-ment was signed, the World Bank, the United States and Great Britain each had pledged loans of about 30 million dollars for the Volta project. At the same time, a group of American and British aluminum interests led by the Kaiser Aluminum Corporation was negotiating for a bauxite mining concession and the construction of an aluminum smelter that would use the bulk of Volta water power.

On top of all this, Ghana's Ambassador in Bonn, Theodore O. Assare, in September negotiated a technical assistance agreement with a consortium of West German engineering firms, including Ferrostaal AG of Essen, Strabag AG of Col-ogne and the Didier Works AG of Wiesbaden. The accord, which was signed on September 23, 1960, stipulates much as the Ghanaian-Soviet agreement did, that the two countries will cooperate in the economic development of the African republic, that the Germans will also lend financial assistance and that native technicians are to be trained in Germany with a view to preparing them for leading positions in the industry of their country. The agreement was described in the German press as a "Rahmenabkommen", or overall compact providing the framework within which individual and specific deals are to be negotiated later on.

However, as in the cases of the U.A.R. and Guinea (see below) Bonn's generous economic assistance to Ghana failed to prevent the DDR from also developing its foothold in that country. Commercial exchanges between the two countries have tripled in three years as the following chart, published in the East German *Foreign Affairs Bulletin* (Nov. 11, 1961), shows:

DDR Trade with African (and some other) Countries:

	Export		Import	
	(in 1,000 dollars)			
	1958	1960	1958	1960
Iraq	663	2,221	35	1,292
Ghana	329	1,122	123	.558
Guinea	1,448°	5,586	1,722°	3,631
Morocco	423	1,246	4,009	1,307
Sudan	1,476	690	3,014	1,947
UAR	25,002	31,341	24,706	30,971
Cuba	131	2,683	473	4,384

°(1959)

On the political level, too, friendly relations prevail. Witness the goodwill telegrams dispatched on July 1, 1962, second anniversary of the Republic of Ghana, to President Nkrumah by Walter Ulbricht and DDR Foreign Minister Lothar Bolz.

Guinea

If President Kwame Nkrumah of Ghana had taken a leaf from Egypt's President Gamal Abdel Nasser in playing off the East against the West and making the best, economically speaking, of both worlds, President Sekou Touré of Guinea, in his turn, followed in the footsteps of Nkrumah. Indeed, almost all that has been said above about the evolution of

Ghana, since it became independent, could be applied also to Guinea without changing much more than a few dates, names and figures. However, the balancing act performed by Sekou Touré on the tightrope stretching from Bonn to Pankow was even more daring and breathtaking than the acrobatics of Messrs. Nasser and Nkrumah.

Literally within hours after Guinea, on October 2, 1958, had proclaimed its independence, severing its last ties to the French "communauté", East Germany wired congratulations and offered to establish diplomatic relations with the new state. While this offer was not immediately taken up — Sekou Touré also had his eyes on West Germany and knew well that the "Hallstein Doctrine" would not permit him to have diplomatic relations with both German states — the congratulations were heartily accepted and warm, if unofficial, contacts followed.

The Bonn Government, for its part, was in no hurry to recognize the new state, for Chancellor Adenauer is always anxious to spare the susceptibilities of his good neighbor, General Charles de Gaulle. Therefore, it was not until after France had indicated that she would reluctantly agree to Guinea's proclamation of independence, that Bonn made the first moves towards the establishment of diplomatic relations. On October 20, 1958, the German consul in Dakar traveled to Conakry to convey his government's congratulations to the newly elected President Touré and his Cabinet. And on October 31, Adenauer, in a telegram to Touré, formally recognized the Republic of Guinea and offered to establish diplomatic relations. However, it was not until January 7, 1959, that a special envoy from Bonn, Dr. Korth, arrived in Conakry; full diplomatic relations between the two countries were not established until July, 1959.

In the meantime, the other side had not been idle either. As early as November 17, 1958, Guinean and East German representatives signed a trade agreement in Conakry, which was followed in December by a cultural accord. In exchange for a goodly portion of Guinea's hard-to-sell (on the world market) crops, in particular, bananas, coffee and oil seeds, the DDR promised to deliver urgently needed machinery, textiles, chemicals and consumer goods. In addition, Pankow invited the Guinean Government to send students and workers to Germany for professional training and offered to send to Guinea experts and specialists in various fields.

By late February, 1959, a well-staffed "Trade Representation of the DDR", headed by Consul-General Wilhelm Kirschei, was functioning in Conakry under the nose of Bonn's special envoy, Dr. Korth, who having arrived only a few weeks earlier was still working in makeshift surroundings. From the start, Herr Kirschei and his staff of about twelve persons enjoyed full diplomatic privileges such as personal immunity and exemption from customs inspection and duties.

After the Pankow Government, in October, 1959, had extended a formal invitation to Sekou Touré to pay a state visit in East Berlin, the newly appointed West German ambassador to Conakry, Dr. Herbert Schröder — he did not actually present his credentials until December, but had been selected for the post some time earlier — urged his government to bestir itself or risk falling behind in its diplomatic contest with the DDR.

As a result, Touré received an invitation from the newly elected President of the Federal Republic, Heinrich Lübke, to visit Bonn (Chancellor Adenauer later used to make the point: "I didn't invite him" — i.e., Touré). Red carpets were rolled out all over for the tall, dark-hued visitor when Touré, between state visits to Washington, London, Paris and Moscow, arrived in Bonn on November 16, 1959, for a four-day tour of the Federal Republic. Amidst a great display of pomp, with military bands playing and honor companies saluting, Touré was received by both President Lübke and Chancellor Adenauer.

However, the practical results of Touré's junket to Bonn were meager. They were far more bountiful on his subsequent visit to Moscow, where the Guinean leader obtained the promise of a 140-million-ruble credit, which was formally granted on March 1, 1960. This mark of Soviet generosity undoubtedly had something to do with the amazing diplomatic comedy that was to follow.

At the beginning of March, 1960, the Bonn Government was stunned by two unexpected diplomatic blows delivered in quick succession by the supposedly friendly, and so recently honored, Sekou Touré. First, on March 1st, the Guinean chargé d'affaires at the United Nations handed to Secretary-General Dag Hammarskjoeld an amazing document: a resolution adopted by the executive committee of the only political party of any consequence in Guinea, the "Democratic Party", which Touré himself had founded in 1946 and whose undisputed leader he remained. Accompanied by a letter from President Touré, this paper assumed in fact, though not formally, the importance of a diplomatic note.

In this note, the Guinean party bluntly accused the Federal Republic on two counts. One was the charge that West Germany had lent France technical and financial assistance in the production of the Sahara atom bomb; the other, that *Bundeswehr* soldiers were fighting with the French Foreign Legion in Algeria. The Bonn Government promptly denied both allegations, which an official spokesman characterized as "monstrous slander".

Even before the West Germans' shock and indignation over this unprovoked attack had subsided, the East German news agency ADN on March 5 announced the establishment of diplomatic relations between the DDR and Guinea. According to this announcement, Guinea's ambassador, Dr. Seydou Conte, had presented his credentials to President Wilhelm Pieck of the DDR and East German ambassador Karl Nohr had taken up his post in Conakry.

To the Bonn Government, which apparently had no inkling of what was brewing, this was bad news indeed. If true, it meant that for the first time a non-Communist state had, in open defiance of the Hallstein Doctrine, granted full recognition to the East German state. Even though Guinea was a small and relatively unimportant country, its move could have far-reaching consequences. Not even Nasser of Egypt had gone quite so far as Sekou Touré had done. If Guinea was allowed to get away with it, the precedent was created and a spate of recognitions of the DDR by the non-committed states might follow.

In the face of this serious challenge, Bonn reacted quickly and forcefully. Its first thought was to break off relations with Guinea forthwith and indeed the Christian Democratic party leadership in the Bundestag recommended such action. On second thought, however, the Adenauer Government decided to make sure that the facts were as they had been represented in East Berlin. Ambassador Schröder was recalled from Conakry for consultations, after telephone inquiries had failed to yield results; and Guinean Ambassador Nabi Youla was summoned from Paris (his headquarters) to Bonn for explanations.

There followed a little game of hide-and-seek unprecedented in diplomatic history. Nabi Youla, in a talk with German Undersecretary of State Hilger von Scherpenberg, on March 8, declared that all he knew about the case was what he had read in the papers. Ambassador Schröder, who was received by Von Scherpenberg the same day, could only report that he had received official confirmation of the establishment of diplomatic relations between Guinea and the DDR.

On March 9, the Bonn Cabinet authorized Foreign Minister Heinrich von Brentano to take all necessary steps, including a diplomatic rupture, unless Guinea "in the shortest possible time" — there was talk of two or at the most three days — gave assurances that the announcement made by East Berlin was false. It was in fact an ultimatum, and it was thus described in parts of the German press even though the official wording was more reserved.

But Sekou Touré nevertheless continued to hedge and evade the issue. He refused to issue a denial on the grounds that he had made no announcement. When he finally did take a stand, he did so in a manner most unpalatable to the Bonn Government. In a talk with a special correspondent of the German newsmagazine *Der Spiegel,* the Guinean President declared what Bonn would have liked to hear officially, namely that no diplomatic relations had been established between his country and the DDR. This was in fact another affront, for *Der Spiegel,* which frequently attacks the Adenauer Government, is anything but popular with the powers-that-be. So, on March 13, a Bonn spokesman sourly commented that remarks made by Sekou Touré to a journalist could hardly be considered a satisfactory reply.

On March 16, Nabi Youla returned to Bonn to hand to Undersecretary Von Scherpenberg a message from Touré to Adenauer. After a 55-minute interview with the German official, the Guinean ambassador told reporters: "The conversation was positive. The existing diplomatic relations between Guinea and West Germany will remain. Guinea has no diplomatic relations with East Germany, but only commercial relations." A spokesman for the Bonn Government, however, was less sanguine about the outcome. "Certain unclear questions remain to be clarified", he declared.

Again, Sekou Touré took his time answering these questions. On March 26, *Die Welt* reported: "With growing impatience, the Federal Government is waiting for the answers to questions it submitted a week ago to Guinea's Chief of State Sekou

Touré ... Bonn would like to have a clear-cut answer to the question whether an ambassador of Guinea has been accredited to East Berlin ..." (In the meantime, it had been learned that Dr. Seydou Conte, who had been received by Wilhelm Pieck on March 5, was Guinea's ambassador to *Moscow*.)

When Sekou Touré continued to procrastinate, Bonn took the bull by the horns. A special emissary, Hasso von Etzdorf, was dispatched to Conakry with orders to find out whether or not an ambassador from the Soviet zone (DDR) was accredited there. When Herr von Etzdorf first arrived at Conakry, on April 3, he learned that President Touré was 450 miles away at Kankan. The German envoy waited paitiently for the President's return. On April 8, Foreign Minister Von Brentano broke into a budget debate of the Bundestag with the happy news that Von Etzdorf had seen Touré and had received the assurances he was looking for. He had learned that East Germany's would-be ambassador, Karl Nohr, had returned home after remaining in Conakry for only fourteen days, and that he had not been received by President Touré.

Bonn now declared itself satisfied, although the formal and written denial which it had demanded from Sekou Touré never materialized. The whole affair, it now was officially explained in Bonn, had been a misunderstanding. When Dr. Conte called on East German President Pieck, he did not present credentials, but merely delivered a document expressing the wish for friendly ties, which the East Germans misinterpreted as diplomatic recognition. The Pankow Government had been "unmasked as liars", wrote the Bonn *Diplomatic Correspondence*, semiofficial organ of the Foreign Office.

So far, so good. But that is not the end of the story yet. For one thing, fact is that the telephone directory of Conakry still lists on page 1, as it has done for some time, "Ambassade de la Republique Democratique Allemande" (Embassy of the German Democratic Republic), which is the official name of the

East German state. For another, the *Hamburger Abendblatt* reported on July 9, 1960: "Guinea's President Sekou Touré has dispatched his brother Mohammed incognito to Bonn on a mission designed to settle the diplomatic conflict with the Federal Republic without publicity." Thus, three months after Bonn had let it be known that the affair was settled, it still remained to be! Also, in September, Sekou Touré again strengthened his ties with the Soviet bloc by visiting Moscow and Peiping and bringing back another 100-million rubles loan — this time from Red China, and without interest at that.

Although Touré subsequently had a serious fall-out with Moscow — he even declared the Soviet ambassador *persona non grata* and sent him home — relations between the DDR and Guinea were not affected by this event. Indeed, East German technicians today are busier in Guinea than in any other part of Africa. They have built, among other things, a powerful radio transmitter and a loudspeaker system which carries the voice of the government to the farthest corners and lowliest huts of Conakry. It is a complex and costly installation that makes it possible for the speaker to address specific streets only, while other areas of the city are switched off.

Late in January, 1962, Consul General Willi Kirschei of the DDR presented to the Guinean ministry of education films, charts, globes and handicraft material for polytechnical training as a "solidarity gift" from the (East) German Institute for Teaching Aids, indicating that relations still are good.

26

Can We Put
Humpty-Dumpty Together
Again?

About six weeks before that fateful August 13, 1961, when The Wall went up in Berlin, making the partition of Germany and the bisection of its former capital, Berlin, a near-permanent fixture of the world situation, an almost funny thing happened. The West German Research Council on Questions of Reunification ("Forschungsbeirat für Fragen der Wiedervereinigung") presented to the Bonn Government a "crash program" of economic measures to be taken on "X-Day" for the purpose of quickly joining the two parts of Germany together again.

It would be difficult to push illusionism and wishful thinking to greater heights of absurdity. Yet the men and women who form the "Research Council on Questions of Reunification" are anything but crackpots or cranks. They are scholars, economists, trade union leaders, businessmen and representatives of the principal political parties in the Bonn Parliament. This Council has semi-official status. It operates under the auspices of the Federal Ministry for All-German Affairs headed by Ernst Lemmer. It has been in existence for some ten years.

The Council's "crash program" recommendations are embodied in a 300-page report which was made public in the early part of July, 1961. There is something truly pathetic about this valiant scientific effort carried out with typical German thoroughness yet based on a quite un-German, indeed a quixotic, disregard for the most elementary realities.

Indeed, one finds in this report, among many other futilities, for instance, a ponderous discussion of the pros and cons of rebuilding the small potteries of Thuringia and other parts of the DDR which had been snuffed out by a regime anxious to concentrate its means and energies on industrial plants of vital importance to the national economy.

Yet the real absurdity of this report does not lie in the many trivial questions it raises. Rather it consists in working out a long list of recommendations — most of them sound and plausible enough by themselves— which are predicated on the complete fallacy of a Germany reunited by peaceful means and on wholly Western terms. For the keynote of the report is that a system of unfettered private enterprise, which the Germans call "Marktwirtschaft" (sometimes with the prefix "social", at other times without it), can be re-established on the territory of what is now the DDR as a result of some sort of new "economic miracle."

These West German day-dreamers who fervently believe reunification is a manna that will fall from heaven tomorrow, if only we pray for it earnestly enough, stubbornly close their eyes to two hard facts: one, that the Kremlin will never permit a destruction of the self-styled Socialist — actually, Communist — economy that has been built in East Germany; and two, that nothing short of total war can budge the Soviets from such a fundamental determination. Total war of course would bring speedy reunification to all Germans — in the greatest mass grave of all history.

Should any thought of reunification then be ruled out forever? By no means. But we in the West must face the reality that it can be achieved only on the basis of mutual concessions and that, if it ever comes about at all, it will be a long historical process.

Are the East German Communists opposed in principle to any thought of reunification? Not at all. For many years they were beating the drums for it almost as hard as the West Germans. Of late, it is true, the clamor has been somewhat more subdued, and that's a good sign. For it means that the Kremlin, for its part, is beginning to realize that it cannot have a Germany reunited on its terms, either.

For, when the rulers of the DDR speak of reunification they of course have in mind a totally different kind of picture from that conceived by the West. They are thinking of a Germany reunited in the form of a "Socialist people's republic", in other words an extension of their present political, economic and social system to the Federal Republic. No doubt somewhere in East Berlin there exists a "Research Council" of Communist dogmatists and economic strategists who are laying elaborate plans for what to do about the Ruhr District on "X-Day."

The basic, primary, inescapable fact of life confronting anyone who gives earnest thought to the question of how to translate the slogans about reunification into a minimum of practical application is this: in the 17 years that have passed since the end of World War II, the two portions of Germany that were carved out by the victors at that time have grown apart more and more politically, economically and socially.

Granted that the difference in popular political sentiment may not be as great as the official positions would indicate. For example, I, too, believe that even now a free election in East Germany would produce a majority in favor of reunification with the Federal Republic on Western terms. And that is precisely why the men presently in power in East Berlin are determined not to give in on the subject of free elections. They would be swept away, and they know it.

For as yet, the genuine and convinced Communists are decidedly in a minority in the DDR. To what extent, no one can tell precisely, for the carefully rigged "elections" provide no clue, and party membership is not a valid criterion either. Still there is little doubt that a completely free and honest count of noses in the DDR at this time would produce a comfortable majority for the non-Communists.

But — and this is a most important "but" that is unfortunately seldom taken into consideration by Western policy makers — the situation is slowly changing in favor of the ruling party. Not only because there has been a marked — and in spite of recurring setbacks, on the whole steady — improvement in living conditions, but also, and most significantly, because in those 17 years a new generation has grown up, a generation spoon-fed on Communist theory and pampered in Communist practice that knows West Germany only from hearsay and the blessings (or evils) of "soziale Marktwirtschaft" not at all. This is a momentous development that is bound to exert a profound influence on the further evolution of the German problem in the years ahead.

However, as yet, the number of people living in the DDR who have grown up under capitalism and have been accustomed to thinking of Germany in terms of a *Reich*, or a nation united in one realm — whether it be the Kaiser's empire, the Weimar Republic or Hitler's totalitarian state — is substantially greater than those who were born or who grew up under the Communist regime. Consider these figures:

At the start of 1960, the total population of the DDR was 17,825,902. Out of this total, 2,670,579 were children under ten years old; 2,558,951 were in the age group from 10 to 21 years; 7,306,831 were grownups in the prime of life (from 21 to 55 years) and 4,749,541 were elderly or old people above the age of 55.

Taking this last age group first, it may be considered one composed of people very set in their views of life and most unlikely to embrace any changes. Among these 4.7 million persons, there are a few leftovers from the era of Imperial Germany; a sizable number of old-style German Liberals and Social-Democrats from the days of the Weimar Republic; many former Nazis and a lot of hard-core Communists. Among the latter are many top figures in the present regime, men like Ulbricht, Grotewohl, Ebert, Warnke, Winzer, Matern and Hilde Bejamin.

How many in this age group would be reliable Communists? Probably not more than 25 to 30 percent. At least the same percentage would go for the irreconcilable (but of course not overt) anti-Communists while the balance of 40 to 50 percent is made up of non-Communists who more or less reluctantly cooperate with the regime.

At the opposite end of the age spectrum — discounting of course the 2.6 million small children for the purposes of this analysis — the proportions would be quite different. Of the younger people, i.e. those 2.5 million in the age brackets 10 to 21, at least 60 to 70 percent are in favor of the present regime while the percentage of those resolutely hostile to it hardly exceeds 10 to 15 percent.

In the largest of the above circumscribed age groups, comprising some 7.3 million people, the picture again is different. A fair guess, it seems to me, would be to put the Communists and sympathizers in this age group at 30 to 40 percent, the all-out enemies of the regime at 15 to 20 percent with the balance made up by opportunists, careerists and the "Wait-and-see" kind of people.

These percentages are of course speculative, even though

based on research and personal observation. Quite possibly some of the figures may be wide of the mark. On the whole, however, they reflect the current trend, I believe.

This trend definitely favors the present regime. For, there can be no doubt that it is being accepted more readily by the young than by the middle-aged or the old. (In a democracy, of course, the opposite occurs, because there is more opportunity for study, a wider scope of vision and greater freedom of expression.)

It follows, then, that a few years hence the regime will be more solidly established than now. As the small fry now in nurseries and kindergartens — and they are very well taken care of, as I have pointed out elsewhere in this book — move into the classrooms to be subjected for ten years or more to methodic and thorough indoctrination, while each year tens of thousands of hard-core opponents pass away, the balance is bound to shift a bit more from one year to the next.

Barring a major war, the chances are that some ten or twenty years hence, the DDR will be as firmly entrenched as is the Soviet Union today, and for the same reason. Because the younger generation then firmly installed in managerial positions or in political authority will never have known nor desired to know the difference of an outside world governed by principles of democracy and free enterprise.

Nor should it be overlooked that the mass exodus of malcontents from the DDR which had been going on until August 13, 1961, and has been so much applauded in the West, actually helped *speed* the same development. For, while it may have weakened the short-run economic potential of the regime, it certainly strengthened its political hold on the people. The fewer opponents, or even grumblers, there are about in any land, the greater and more unchallenged is the power of the government.

All this, then, leads inevitably to the conclusion that the SED-controlled regime, which is far stronger today than it was in 1953, the year of the great popular upheaval against it, will be even stronger ten years from now. It is not at all impossible that by that time it will be in a position mockingly to organize the free elections it now so stubbornly refuses to hold, confident that the well-indoctrinated and on the whole satisfied young men and women who by 1972 will have attained voting age will give it a firm majority in parliament.

Maybe I am too pessimistic, but I can't help feeling the hopeful idea, much cherished in the West, that the young people of Eastern Germany will somehow have inherited an instinct of freedom, democracy and private enterprise and will show themselves deeply attached to it when the time comes, springs from sheer illusionism.

If the political facts of life and the social trends now at work do not favor smooth reunification, the obstacles in the economic field appear well-nigh insurmountable. Significantly, the "Research Council on Questions of Reunification", in its above-cited report, carefully dodges the basic question confronting it; what to do about the collectivized farmland, the expropriated real estate, the nationalized industries, the state-run hotels, businesses, stores, restaurants, etc., etc.

It will indeed be a herculean task, fraught with dangers and pitfalls, to try to restore these to the former owners, or to distribute them among other private individuals. There is no historical precedent of a firmly entrenched Socialist economy being returned to private hands and I doubt that it can be done successfully. At best such a process would probably take decades and would engender a veritable rat's-tail of legal complications and lawsuits.

On the other hand, it seems just as inconceivable that two such fundamentally divergent economic systems as the "freie Marktwirtschaft" of Western Germany and the Socialist (or

Communist) "Staatswirtschaft" of Eastern Germany could peacefully and efficiently operate side by side within the same country, à la federation of states like West Germany.

What, then, is the answer? Is some form of reunification possible without one of the two Germanies now in existence swallowing the other and crushing its political system?

While the West Germans steadfastly refuse even to contemplate any solution of the German problem other than the unconditional absorption of the DDR into the political and economic system of the Federal Republic, the Ulbricht regime of late has been talking a great deal about "confederation." It would like the two German states now in existence to form a loose partnership in which each of them would retain complete control of its internal affairs and foreign policy, as a transitional stage that might eventually lead to reunification.

Is such a course possible?

I doubt it very much indeed. It would be like an attempt to confederate fire and water, or iceberg and volcano.

In order to become anything more than a pretense, even the loosest form of confederation presupposes that the partners have something more in common than just the language. And just that is not the case.

How can anyone imagine a German Confederation, like Janus looking in opposite directions at the same time, practicing foreign defense and trade policies that are not only incompatible but resolutely opposed to each other? No — this suggestion is absurd on the face of it and one cannot blame the West Germans for turning it down.

Let us face the reality of the situation, bitter as it may taste to patriotic Germans in both camps: reunification is improbable in the foreseeable future. Nothing but a fundamental shift in the present balance of power could open up an avenue leading towards it. And such a shift just isn't anywhere in sight.

What is quite practicable, by contrast, with a minimum of peaceful intentions and good will, is a modus vivendi or standstill agreement under which each of the two states would be committed to the elementary courtesies of neighborhood.

It was General Lucius D. Clay, President Kennedy's personal representative in Berlin, hero of the 1948-49 airlift and a man no one in his right mind could accuse of being unsympathetic to the West German cause, who at a famous "off-the-record" press conference, on September 22, 1961, summed up the present situation in these words: "Right now there are two German states, one of which will not talk to the other..."

The one that won't talk to the other is, of course, the Federal Republic. The DDR has been willing to talk all along, that is a fact.

But even if they are not on speaking terms, the Federal Republic and the DDR have consistently maintained so-called "technical contacts" in such matters as postal service, interzonal trade, road and railroad traffic, shipping, etc. Even at the darkest moments of crisis, the mail has gone through unimpeded from one Germany to the next and trade relations never came to a full stop.

This may come as a surprise to many, but it is a fact nevertheless: Not even the much-lamented, hotly denounced building of the intra-city wall in Berlin interfered *in the least* with West-East German trade relations.

"Intrazonal Trade in 1961 Without Setback" ran a banner headline in the *Deutsche Zeitung* of Cologne and Stuttgart on December 27, 1961. In the text of the article, the paper, which is close to West German industrial circles and in its editorial outlook decidedly unfriendly to the East German regime, noted that the total volume of intra-zonal trade in 1961, in spite of an apparent shrinkage of 7.3 percent, actually remained at the same level as before. It amounted to 1.49 billion

"Verrechnungseinheiten" ("Clearing units")* for the first ten months of 1961, as compared to 1.6 billion in the same period of 1960, but this ostensible decrease actually resulted from technicalities, the paper explained. Not only was there no genuine diminution of trade, but in October a trend towards intensified exchanges set in which made it appear likely that the totals for the whole year would be even better than for 1960.

In the present world situation, the only practical approach towards the German problem must start out from these existing technical contacts and trade relations which can be enlarged and improved. Also, they could and should be placed on a somewhat higher level of authority than the rather subordinate one on which they are now being conducted.

Cultural exchanges also should be expanded or at least resumed. If the United States and the Soviet Union can improve their cultural relations to the extent noticeable in the early months of 1962, why should not the Federal Republic and the DDR, which are just as far apart politically and ideologically, but at least have a common language and to a great extent share the same history and cultural legacies, be able to do so?

Maybe the psychological moment has not yet come for diplomatic relations between the two German states; maybe it won't come for a long time. But the search for a modus vivendi must never stop.

In the atomic age, there is no alternative to peaceful coexistence.

---

*Because of the large actual disparity in value between West marks and East marks (more than 4:1 on the average), which is not, however, recognized officially by the East German regime, trade between the Federal Republic and the DDR is carried on exclusively on the basis of these artificial currency units.